The BEHOLD METHOD

BIBLICAL STUDY

Learn to study the Bible like seminarians.

Transform your quiet time.

behold

INTRO

If written Bible studies aren't your thing, or you'd rather dig into Scripture with just the Holy Spirit, your Bible, paper, pens, and markers, this is the Method for you.

With methods that seminarians, Bible teachers, Bible curriculum writers, and preachers have been using for years, you will be able to open your Bible and know exactly what to look for, and how to apply it to your own life.

Beyond verse mapping, you'll learn how to dissect entire passages of Scripture, whatever size you want.

So, grab your fave drink, decide on a time to make a daily appointment with Jesus and come along!

TABLE OF CONTENTS

About the Behold Collective

The Behold Method

Observe.

Interpret.

Connect.

Apply.

BEHOLD. BELIEVE.
BEFRIEND.
"Become the woman God
created you to be!"
@thebeholdcollective

ABOUT THE
behold

COLLECTIVE

Every time you see the word "behold" in the Bible, pay attention to what comes after it. Behold in the Hebrew Bible acts like an exclamation mark. So, take note!

The Behold Collective was founded by Meg Elizabeth Brown in 2020 when she saw a need for discipleship and Bible study material in churches around her. She began collaborating with other believing women whom God had gifted with the same passions, and the Behold Collective was formed. They have written many discipleship workshops, Biblical training sessions, Bible studies, blogs, free resources, and podcasts, all based around the Behold (God) Moments in Scripture and Behold Moments in our own lives.

Our Vision

Live How God Designed You
We are a collective of women who disciple others to find their identity in Christ, live out their unique purpose, and continue to relationally disciple other women ,

Our Mission

We equip women to discover their identity as they encounter God, emulate Jesus, engage with the Holy Spirit, and teach others to do the same.

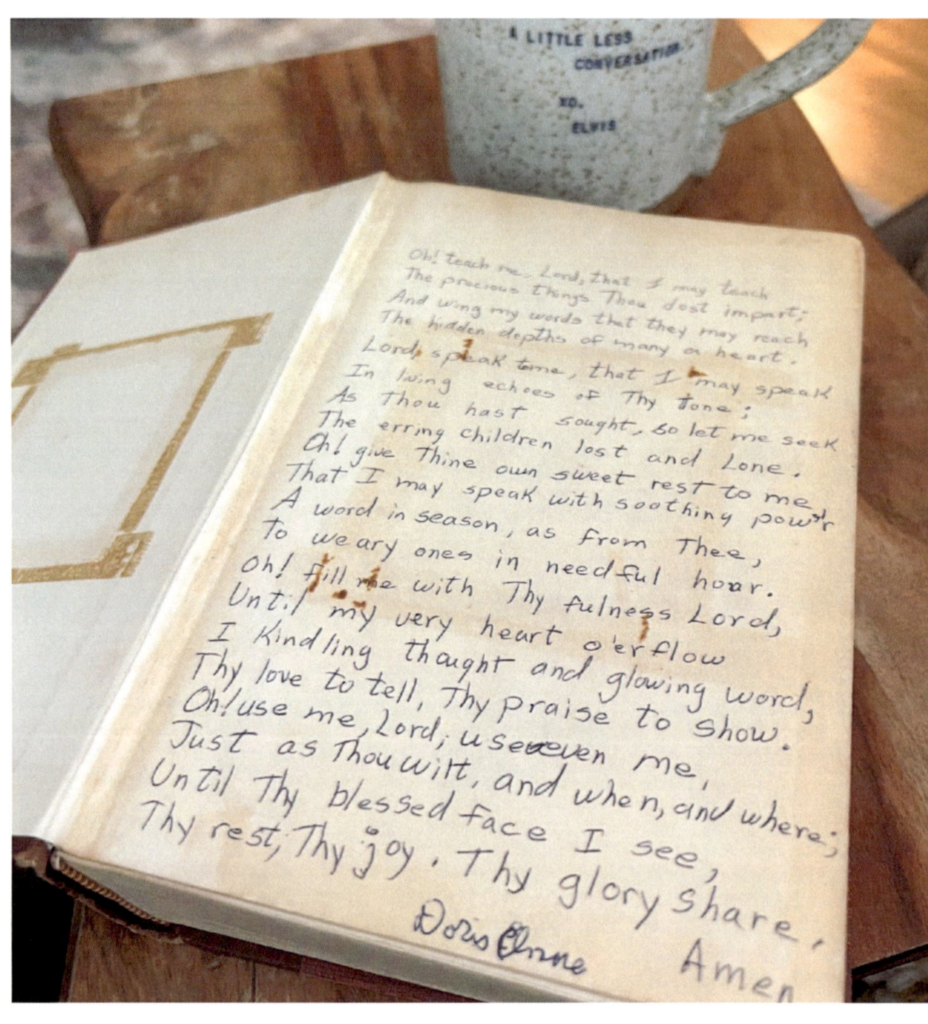

CORE VALUES &
OUR DAILY PURPOSE

With our core values of faith, growth, collaboration, challenge, and relationships we hope to help women understand their true identity made in God's image and learn to follow after Jesus daily. We focus on discipleship and educating women on the intricacies in Scripture and the life-giving intimacy it brings to their relationship with Jesus.

We exist to help women behold their Creator, believe in Jesus, befriend the Holy Spirit, and become the women that God has created them to be.

www.thebeholdcollective.com

BECOME THE WOMAN GOD CREATED YOU TO BE.

IDENTITY

Women who don't fully understand what it means to be made in God's image always feel "too much" or "not enough." If you can fully absorb that YOU are CREATED in GOD'S IMAGE, then you are on your way to knowing WHO you are.

Here at the Behold Collective, we stress how important it is to understand what it means to be created in the image of God. When you understand this simple, but complex fact, you will never question again who God created you to be.

OUR METHODS

When discipling or even studying in your personal devotion time with the Lord, how you study will change depending on your season of life. Choose from one of the methods we recommend and download from our website.

The Swedish Study Method
#01

Perfect for discipling a small group of 2-4 women, but also great for a quick study during your personal study time with the Lord.

The Behold Method
#02

If wanting a more intense, very thorough way of studying the Bible, this is it. You'll learn how to ask questions of the text and learn how to apply it to yourself and your life.

Return to the Garden Series
#03

This study was designed around discipleship. It's great for a mature believer to walk through with a new believer.

So What? Now What?
#04

Another simple and effective method of studying Scripture. This method takes almost no prep and is easy to do in a pinch. It helps you digest giant chunks of information and wrap up how to apply it.

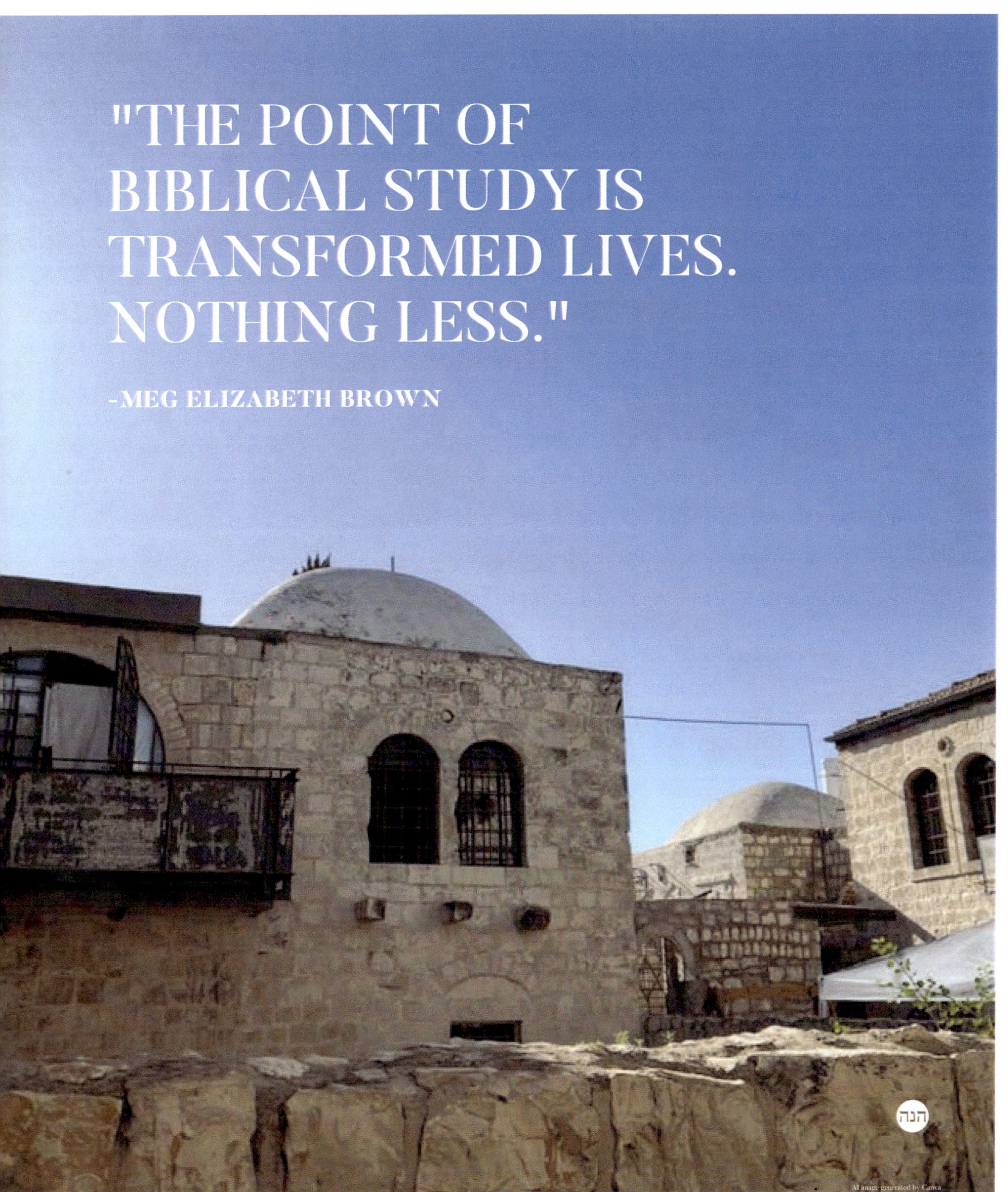
"THE POINT OF BIBLICAL STUDY IS TRANSFORMED LIVES. NOTHING LESS."

-MEG ELIZABETH BROWN

AI image generated by Canva

BEHOLD METHOD

There are many methods that have been developed over the years for personalized Bible study. Here at the Behold Collective, we would rather the biblical text teach us, than to hear from another person's opinion on the text. The Behold Method uses an inductive study method, which is a strategic way to understand and apply Scripture. There are four main areas that it focuses on: observation, interpretation, connection, and application. You will essentially exegete the text to find meaning.

To draw the meaning out of the text
– EXEGESIS

The Behold Method starts with the passage of Scripture and allows the text to speak for itself.

Instead of answering questions from another person's point of view (like a biblical commentary or deductive method of study), the Behold Method teaches you how to ask questions of the text, which allows God to speak to YOU!

AIM: Author's Intended Meaning

The entire point of Biblical study is to discover the author's intended meaning for a particular audience in a particular place at a particular time. Once discovered, you can interpret its meaning for today. In order to understand the A.I.M. of every passage, we must look to see what the author's cultural, historical, and literary context they are writing from. When was it written? Who were they writing to? What is the historical and literary reason for this writing?

THEME & CONTEXT

Look at the surrounding verses of the passage to determine the verses immediate context. Then compare it to the entire chapter... then the book itself. What is the context of the verse in light of these things? Don't allow a verse to stand alone.

BOOK THEME

SURROUNDING CHAPTERS

IMMEDIATE VERSES

VERSE

WHAT IS THE BOOK'S GENRE?

There are several types of literary genre found in the Bible. Make sure you know what genre you're reading. Is it prophecy? Narrative? Law? Remembering where you are in the Bible will help you to interpret it.

BEHOLD METHOD

01 Observe

The first step in this method is to NOTICE what's in the text itself. What does the text say? As Phyllis Bennett of Western Seminary said, "Observation is the art of seeing what is there and its significance. What should you observe?" *

02 Interpret

The second step in this method is to determine what the text means. We must determine what the author meant when they wrote the passage and how the original audience would have understood the passage of scripture. We need to turn away from applying our own modern application upon the text. Dr. Todd L. Miles said, "The Bible was written by a particular author in a particular place at a particular time to a particular people in a particular context."*

How we interpret must depend on the original author's intended meaning for the original audience. We can rely upon the Holy Spirit to guide and help us to interpret the passage through taking off our Western lens and paradigm.

*Phyllis Bennett, Developing Life-Changing Bible Study Curriculum, (Phyllis R. Bennett, 2018), 14.
Todd L. Miles, "BT501 Lecture Notes," BT501 Hermenutetics class at Western Seminary, Spring 2021, 21.

03 Connect

The third step is to connect the text to other biblical texts, cultures, and our lives. Our Bible is a hyperlinked book where biblical sections and verses connect to other areas in the Bible. It is also alive and active and can connect to ancient cultures and our lives today. You'll need to ask questions on how this passage relates to other Scripture, areas of culture, and to yourself and your relationships.

04 Apply

The final step in the Behold Method is application: learning what the text means to you. The goal of Bible study is for the words of God to transform our lives and the lives of those around us. The reason for application is so that our lives reflect the words we say we believe. Our walk must mirror our talk. As Howard Hendricks said, "The object of Bible study is changed lives. The Christian world is suffering from a deficiency of Vitamin A-Application."* Just like Paul wrote in Titus 1:1 (N.I.V.), the Bible is the "truth that leads to godliness."

*Howard Hendricks, Living by the Book," (Chicago, IL: Moody Publishers, 2007).

BOOKEND WITH PRAYER

The minute you open your Bible to begin studying, start with prayer.

At the core of our faith, prayer is what links and connects us to the Father. Without this link, our relationship and faith will not continue to grow and flourish. Prayer is pretty much the first step for everything within the Christian faith.

As a guide, you can follow either the Lord's Prayer or the ACTS prayer. The ACTS prayer is an acrostic for Adoration, Confession, Thanksgiving, and Supplication (asking for your needs). Before diving into the Word, spend some time with Him, and open yourself up to the Holy Spirit's guidance. If you'd like, use the guide on the next page to write out your prayer if you like.

PRAY

Adoration

____

Confession

____

Thanksgiving

____

Supplication

____

Biblical study can be easy.

It just takes dedication, a willingness of
spirit, and time intentionally set aside.

observe

OBSERVE

Six Questions

We first start with six questions to ask the text. They are 5 Ws (**Who, What, Where, When, Why**) and 1 H (**How**).

Key Words

Scour the text for keywords that stand out, repeat, or seem important to the main message of the text.

Differences

Look through the text for ideas that disagree or thoughts or phrases that oppose each other. Words to hone in on this are: **but, however, although, either/or, rather, and yet.**

Similarities

Look for ideas, words, or phrases that point to similar ideas. You'll find these in areas that have words like: **as, just as, also, so, and, like, likewise, the same as.**

Broad to Narrow

Look for movements from broad ideas to narrow, and vice versa. Hebrews 11 is a good example of this where the author is giving examples of faithful people and then concludes with the statement, "the world was not worthy of them." Hebrews 11:38

OBSERVE

Cause and Effect

Look for conclusions or summaries within the passage in question. What is it summarizing? Look for words like: therefore, then, consequently, so that, for this reason, wherefore, finally, so then, if, or if/then. There are also cases where the effect comes before the cause: look for words like: for, due to, and because.

Journey to the End Point

Look for themes that are built upon with details, insights, additional thoughts, descriptions or clarifications. James 1:15 is a good example of this: "After desire is conceived, it gives birth to sin, and sin, when it is full-grown gives birth to death."

Lists

Simple enough? Please be sure to look for lists centered around a specific topic. Other lists look more like "how-to" or things to count.

Behold Moments

Seminarians call it, "cruciality": where the narrative involves a shift in direction, a radical reversal, a turning point because of a pivot passage or word. Look for shifts in the narrative, or the word, "BEHOLD!".

Sum It Up

Review everything you've learned from your observation and try to write a summarizing main idea.

OBSERVE

Six Questions

Who:

What:

Where:

When:

Why:

How:

Key Words

Differences

Similarities

OBSERVE

Broad to Narrow

Cause and Effect

Journey to the End Point

Lists

Behold Moments

Sum It Up

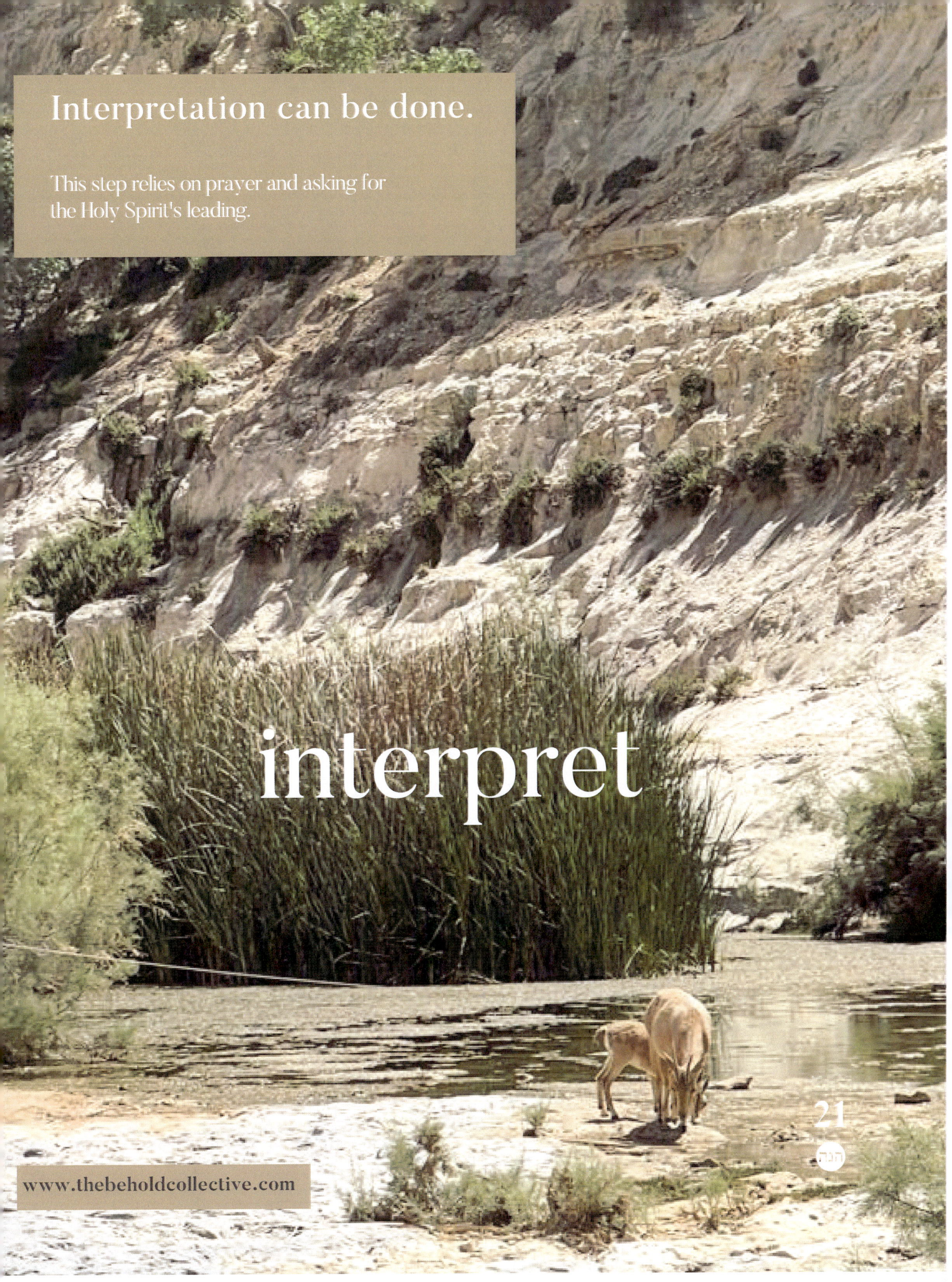

Interpretation can be done.

This step relies on prayer and asking for
the Holy Spirit's leading.

interpret

21

www.thebeholdcollective.com

INTERPRET

Pray

Before interpretation, always begin in prayer. Ask for the Holy Spirit's guidance to lead you to understand the passage.

Backdrop

Make sure you take into account the setting that the passage is found in. Look at the context within the passage, the literary form (is this a narrative, letter, or revelation?), and its historical and cultural setting. Take a peek at pg. 11 to remind yourself of these things.

Context. Context. Context.

Look at its surrounding context (start with chapter before and after) and then put yourself back in time (as best you can) to their time period, culture, and soceital norms. Most false interpretations are due to missing this step.

A.I.M.

What is the "Author's Intended Meaning?" Put this before you jump to define it for our time period and culture.

Literal or Figurative?

Are the words/phrases being used in a literal or figurative way? Look for allegory or figures of speech. Otherwise, lean towards literal interpretation.

INTERPRET

Word Studies

Pay attention to repeated words or words you are unsure of their meaning. Look it up in a Bible dictionary, or find out the word in the original language. Find other places in Scripture where this word (in its original language) is used, where else the author uses it, and in both the Old and New Testament. See page 26 for more.

Grammar

Look at verb tenses, whether it's singular or plural, and especially what the subject and main idea are.

Hyperlinks

Find other Scriptures (some are listed in your Bible as references) that link together. Find ones that are similar in support, help clarify, or expand upon an idea. The Bible is the best interpreter of itself. There are so many hyperlinks that pull us back to other Scripture. Use it! Use a concordance if your Bible doesn't have references.

Historical vs. Teaching

As yourself if what's being discussed was a historical/cultural issue that was being addressed at that time, or is it relevant for teaching today?

INTERPRET

Old and New

Use the Old Testament to help interpret things not understood in the New Testament, and vice versa. Example: understanding the Last Supper in light of what Passover looked like for Israel at that time.

Obvious vs. Obscure

Use the obviously clear passages to help you interpret the obscure ones. (Example: The Exodus is used by other writers like Hosea.)

Tradition

Are you leaning towards one interpretation because of church tradition? Remember, church history does not have the final word. God's Word does. Just because a church denomination believes one thing about a passage, does not make it 100% accurate. We are humans. We make mistakes all the time.

Essential Questions

- Why is this here?
- Why did God lead the author to write this?
- What truth withstands time?
- What does it say about the Trinity?
- What does it say about humanity?
- What does it say about sin or evil?
- What does it say about outlooks on life?
- What about examples?
- What does it say truth is?

INTERPRET

Main Idea

As Nacho Libre said, "Let's get down to the nitty-gritty." What is the MAIN idea in the passage? Remember, there may be additional points or complemntary ones as well. But what's the main one?

Ask Questions of the Text

Begin a list of questions you have that haven't been answered.

Check Outside Resources

Let me stress this: as a last resort, if you're stumped, check commentaries and other sources that you trust to help you interpret a difficult passage. Sit in their interpretations and pray over them. Allow the Holy Spirit to help you discern the truth.

WORD STUDIES

What's a Word Study?

It's digging into the meaning behind a word in a passage as accurately as possible using resources like Bible dictionaries, Bible study software or encyclopedias, original language lexicons, and different translations of the Bible. (See resources to choose from below.)

Why does this matter?

Words change meanings depending on the context and even over time. Finding the original meaning is like finding buried treasure and connecting our hearts to God!

Which word do I pick?

Which word piques your interest? Which word is unfamiliar? Which word is repeated over and over? Look at keywords, nouns, and adjectives. Look at deep theological concepts in the passage and determine if it's worth looking into. Which words do you think, if you fully understood them, would expose the entire passage to the light?

Resources to Choose From

- LOGOs Bible software
- Bible Study Tools (www.biblestudytools.com)
- Blue Letter Bible (www.blueletterbible.com)
- Strong's Exhaustive Concordance (NIV translation)
- The Englishman's Concordance by George V. Wigram
- The Complete Word Study Old and New Testament by Dr. Spiros Zodhiates Th.D. (NASB version)
- Vines Complete Expository Dictionary of Old and New Testament Words

WORD STUDIES

Word Study Steps

1. Look up the word in your Bible software or Bible study website. For example, find the Strong's Concordance number of your word. Write down your summary.
2. Use the Strong's number* to locate all possible definitions(s). In what other ways has this word been defined?
3. Read and compare passages that contain this exact word.
4. Find all the times this word is used in the book of the Bible where your word is located.
5. Find and compare all the times the word is used by the same genre or author (if possible).

Warnings on Interpretation

1. Context. Context. Context. Context ALWAYS matters. It is KING in interpretation. The context will help you determine the best summarizing definition for your word.
2. Once you've finished your work on the word study, find a trusted author who has written on the passage you're studying, or check a trusted Bible commentary to confirm your findings.
3. Other scholars' work can also guide you in knowing literary, historical, and grammatical understandings.
4. Scripture can say whatever you want it to say (if you manipulate it). So BE CAREFUL.

*Strong's Concordance

INTERPRET

- Pray:

- Back Drop:

- Context. Context. Context:

- A.I.M:

INTERPRET

● Literal or Figurative?

● Word Study:

● Grammar:

● Hyperlinks:

● Historical vs. Teaching:

הנה

INTERPRET

● Old and New:

● Obvious vs. Obscure:

● Tradition:

● Essential Questions:

● Main Idea:

INTERPRET

- Ask Questions of the Text:

- Outside Resources:

After a while, it seems as if everything in the Bible is connected. No joke.

-Meg Elizabeth Brown

CONNECT

Connection is extremely important in studying and understanding God's Word. Nothing stands alone. God has woven parallels, rewinds, repeats, and purposeful returns into His Word to get our attention. Not only does His Word connect with itself, but it connects to their culture and reflects into our own lives and culture. His Word is all about connection, which transfers into our relationships in the body of Christ, the Church. So, let these connections in His Word remind you to make connections within and outside the body of Christ, building relationships and discipleship.

CONNECT

Similar Scripture

1. How does this passage connect with other passages of Scripture?
2. Look for parallels and intentional echoes in other passages with similar wording, purposeful word choice, etc (Sometimes this is listed in your Bible's margins!)
3. If you find a theme in the Old Testament (say, a garden, any tree, or water), follow it into the New Testament.
4. If you find a theme in the New Testament, see if you can find a similar theme in the Old.
5. Connect Biblical figures and see how they contrast or compare. How do some figures point to Jesus?

Cultural Crossover

1. Look at the historical-cultural context (from your previous interpretation step) and see if it can connect with your own cultural context. Do the same principles and commands apply? Look at the passage's connection to our culture's areas:
   a. Financial and Production
   b. Body and Flesh
   c. Mental and Emotional
   d. Fun, Athletics, and Hobbies
   e. Desires and Sex
   f. Community and Relational
   g. Beliefs and Ideas
   h. Government and Diplomacy
2. How does this relate to men's and women's issues today?

CONNECT

Reflective

1. How can this passage connect to our past relationships? Check out a more extensive list on the following page.
   a. Family
      i. Spouse and Children
      ii. Parents
      iii. Siblings
      iv. Extended Family
   b. Friends
   c. Neighbors and Neighborhood
   d. Community
   e. Nation
   f. Co-Workers
   g. Globally
2. How can this passage connect to our present relationships? An example: "How does this passage relate to your own life?"
3. What from this passage do you need to apply back to your own life today? What convicted you? What exposed a sin pattern or wrong belief from the passage? Personalize an action item for yourself and follow through.
4. As you read through this passage, did God bring someone to mind? Do you need to share this passage with them this week? What from this passage can you share with someone to bring them joy and peace or deepen their faith? What conviction did this passage bring up that you need to ask for accountability from someone?

THEMES

When looking at Scripture, we need to find connections to our culture and the problems we face today. Look for these themes in order to find ways to apply the passage to your life today.

Passions

- Nutrition
- Physical health and fitness
- Home/Work Balanace
- Hobbies
- Studying God's Word
- Prayer
- Design
- Administration
- Shopping
- Wealth management

Aspirations

- Self-image
- Developing spiritual gifts
- Past mistakes overcome
- Communication
- Organization
- Simplicity
- Prayer
- Memorization of God's Word
- Physical health and fitness
- Managing household, time, and personal interests
- Stewarding the resources and time God has given
- Legacy

Relationships

- Friendship
- Long-time friendship
- Loneliness
- Singleness
- Married life
- Single parenting
- Co-parenting and discipline
- Losing a friend
- Losing a spouse
- Pregnancy and childbirth
- Preschool days
- Blended families
- Teen years
- College and career age
- Empty nesters
- Becoming grandparents
- Marriage help
- Changes in marriage
- Marrying early or later
- Putting your marriage first
- In-law relationships
- Elder care
- Work relationships
- Working with the opposite sex
- Workplace competition
- Faith at work
- Balancing work and home life

Grief and Pain

- Psychological Problems
- Stress and Anxiety
- Trauma
- Choosing Wisdom over Folly
- Substance Abuse
- Abuse towards others
- Emotional Issues
- Mental Conditions
- Crisis Situations
- Sexual Addictions
- Cultural Arguments
- Discontentment
- Caring for caregivers
- Sickness and Pain
- Death and Dying
- Tragedies to those we love
- Loving Addicts
- Recovery and Rehab
- Sexual crimes
- Abuse: physical, mental, emotional and verbal

CONNECT

Similar Scripture:

Culture Crossover:

CONNECT

Reflective

"Without
application, there is
no point to the
story of Jesus."

• Meg Elizabeth Brown

apply

APPLY

APPLY

If we stop after observing, interpreting, and connecting, everything is pointless that we've learned. It's not until we've applied what we've learned that knowledge transfers into wisdom. The word "shema" in Hebrew means to look, listen, and obey. Once we look and listen to what God's Word says, we must obey it. Otherwise, we have not fully finished the loop of Biblical study.

APPLY

What's the Point?

1. Obedience of God's Word brings a change of heart and life choices. What is the passage asking you to change?
2. We cannot just keep the knowledge without acting upon it. What knowledge needs to be applied to your life?
3. It helps you, as the reader, try to find the application that the author intended for his audience. What did the author intend as the application?
4. Make sure the application reaches your heart and not just your head. What touches your heart in this passage?

What to Do?

1. This must be attainable, not reaching for the stars. What is one thing you could do in a period of time, like a week or a month?
2. Make sure to tell someone so that you can be held accountable for what you decide to do or change due to the passage.
3. Check-in with yourself or someone else to take personal accountability for this goal.

APPLY

What's the Point?

What to Do?

BOOKEND WITH PRAYER

As you close your study for today, make sure to finish the conversation with the Father.

After working through your study time, spend some time once again at the feet of the Father. Following a similar model to the ACTS prayer, focus on praising God for His Word, confessing any convictions the text brought out in your own life, thanking Him for what it taught you, and asking for wisdom in the coming studies.

As a guide, you can follow either the Lord's Prayer or the ACTS prayer. The ACTS prayer is an acrostic for Adoration, Confession, Thanksgiving, and Supplication (asking for your needs). Before diving into the Word, spend some time with Him, and open yourself up to the Holy Spirit's guidance. Use the guide on the next page to write out your prayer if you like.

BEHOLD METHOD

PRAY

- Adoration/Praise for God's Word:

- Confession and Conviction:

- Thanks for God's Word:

- Supplication/ Ask for Wisdom:

BEHOLD METHOD

"Memories are the key not to the past, but to the future. I know that the experiences of our lives, when we let God use them, become the mysterious and perfect preparation for the work He will give us to do."
—Corrie ten Boom

הנה

PRAY

- Adoration:

- Confession:

- Thanksgiving:

- Supplication:

OBSERVE

- ## Six Questions:

  Who?

  What?

  Where?

  When?

  Why?

  How?

- ## Key Words:

- ## Differences:

- ## Similarities:

OBSERVE
Broad to Narrow

Cause and Effect

Journey to the End Point

Lists

Behold Moments

Sum It Up

INTERPRET

- Pray:
  ____

- Back Drop:
  ____

- Context. Context. Context:
  ____

- A.I.M:
  ____

INTERPRET

- Literal or Figurative?

- Word Study:

- Grammar:

- Hyperlinks:

- Historical vs. Teaching:

INTERPRET

- Old and New:

- Obvious vs. Obscure:

- Tradition:

- Essential Questions:

- Main Idea:

הנה

INTERPRET

Ask Questions of the Text:

Outside Resources:

CONNECT

Similar Scripture:

Culture Crossover:

CONNECT

Reflective:

APPLY

What's the Point?

What to Do?

APPLY

PRAY

● Praise for God's Word:

● Confession and Conviction:

● Thanks for God's Word:

● Ask for Wisdom:

"When you read the Bible, you must think that here and now,
God is speaking with me."
-Dietrich Bonhoeffer-

Place Value Chart

Millions	1,000,000	**Decimals**	
Hundred-Thousands	100,000	Tenths	0.1
Ten-Thousands	10,000	Hundredths	0.01
Thousands	1,000	Thousandths	0.001
Hundreds	100		
Tens	10		
Ones	1		

Each place is **10**× the place to its right, and $\frac{1}{10}$ of the place to its left.

Key Math Vocabulary

- **Sum** — the result of addition
- **Difference** — the result of subtraction
- **Product** — the result of multiplication
- **Quotient** — the result of division
- **Remainder** — what's left over after dividing
- **Factor** — a number you multiply
- **Expression** — numbers and operations without =
- **Equation** — a math sentence with =
- **Numerator** — the top number of a fraction
- **Denominator** — the bottom number of a fraction
- **Mixed number** — a whole number + a fraction
- **Equivalent fractions** — fractions with equal value
- **Decimal** — a number written with a decimal point
- **Volume** — the space inside a 3D shape
- **Coordinate plane** — a grid with x and y axes
- **Ordered pair** — (x, y) location on the plane

Word Problem Clue Words

- **Add** (+): total, altogether, combined, sum, increase, more than
- **Subtract** (−): difference, how many more, fewer, remain, decrease, left
- **Multiply** (×): each, every, groups of, times, product, per, of (with fractions)
- **Divide** (÷): share equally, split, each group, how many groups, quotient, per

▦ Multiplication Table ▦

You may use this table during your practice tests!

×	1	2	3	4	5	6	7	8	9	10	11
1	1	2	3	4	5	6	7	8	9	10	11
2	2	4	6	8	10	12	14	16	18	20	22
3	3	6	9	12	15	18	21	24	27	30	33
4	4	8	12	16	20	24	28	32	36	40	44
5	5	10	15	20	25	30	35	40	45	50	55
6	6	12	18	24	30	36	42	48	54	60	66
7	7	14	21	28	35	42	49	56	63	70	77
8	8	16	24	32	40	48	56	64	72	80	88
9	9	18	27	36	45	54	63	72	81	90	99
10	10	20	30	40	50	60	70	80	90	100	110
11	11	22	33	44	55	66	77	88	99	110	121

💡 How to Use This Table

To find **4 × 7**:

1. Find **4** in the left column (blue).
2. Find **7** in the top row (blue).
3. Follow the row and column until they meet: the answer is **28**!

ⓘ Tip: You can also use this table for division! If you know 28 ÷ 4 = ?, find 28 in the 4's row. The column header gives you the answer: **7**!

🏢 Construction Log 🏢

Record each floor and watch your tower rise

Architect: _________________________________   Project Start: _________________

Phase I: Foundation — Floors 1–3

📐 **Floor 1**   Date: _________   Score: _____ / _____   %: _____   ☆☆☆☆☆
📐 **Floor 2**   Date: _________   Score: _____ / _____   %: _____   ☆☆☆☆☆
📐 **Floor 3**   Date: _________   Score: _____ / _____   %: _____   ☆☆☆☆☆

Phase II: Framework — Floors 4–6

📐 **Floor 4**   Date: _________   Score: _____ / _____   %: _____   ☆☆☆☆☆
📐 **Floor 5**   Date: _________   Score: _____ / _____   %: _____   ☆☆☆☆☆
📐 **Floor 6**   Date: _________   Score: _____ / _____   %: _____   ☆☆☆☆☆

Phase III: Finishing — Floors 7–9

📐 **Floor 7**   Date: _________   Score: _____ / _____   %: _____   ☆☆☆☆☆
📐 **Floor 8**   Date: _________   Score: _____ / _____   %: _____   ☆☆☆☆☆
📐 **Floor 9**   Date: _________   Score: _____ / _____   %: _____   ☆☆☆☆☆

Phase IV: Capstone — Floor 10

📐 **Floor 10**   Date: _________   Score: _____ / _____   %: _____   ☆☆☆☆☆

Certification Level: Apprentice (0–39%)   Technician (40–59%)   Engineer (60–79%)   **Master Architect** (80–100%)

Record your certification level after each test!

Under Construction

____

____

____

____

Construction Complete

★ ____

★ ____

★ ____

★ ____

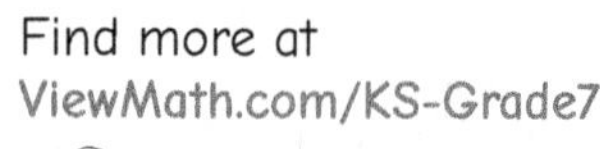

Find more at
ViewMath.com/KS-Grade7

⭐ Table of Contents ⭐

Here's what we'll explore together!

Let's learn and have fun!

Practice Test 1

30 Questions

✏️ Before You Start ✏️

- ✔ **Read each question carefully** before choosing your answer.
- ✔ **Show your work** on scratch paper when you need to.
- ✔ **Skip hard questions** and come back to them later.
- ✔ **Check your answers** when you're done.
- ✔ **Take your time** — there's no rush!

⭐ You've Got This! ⭐

Do your best and show what you know!

1. The table shows a proportional relationship. Find k and the missing value.

x	y
3	7.5
?	15
10	25

Your Answer

2. Two proportional lines are graphed below. Which statement is correct?

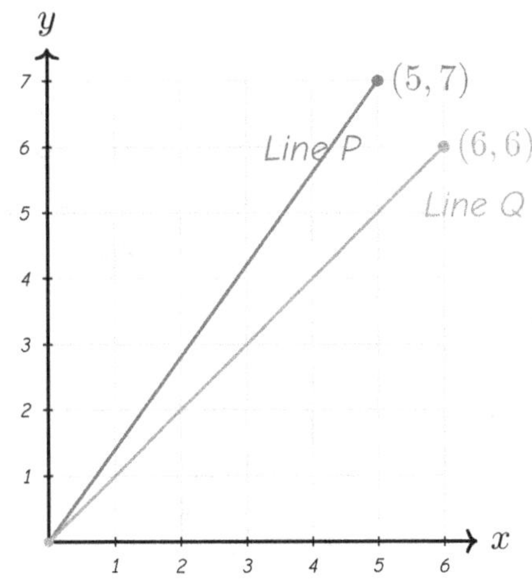

(A) Line Q has the greater unit rate because it is longer

(B) Line P has the greater unit rate because it is steeper

(C) Both lines have the same unit rate

(D) Line Q has the greater unit rate because $6 > 5$

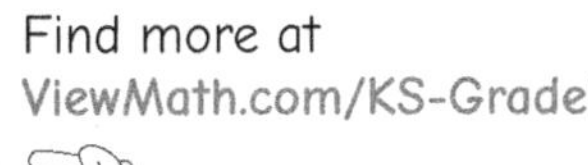

Find more at
ViewMath.com/KS-Grade7

3. *The graph below compares the rates of two workers packaging boxes. Which worker is faster, and by how many boxes per hour?*

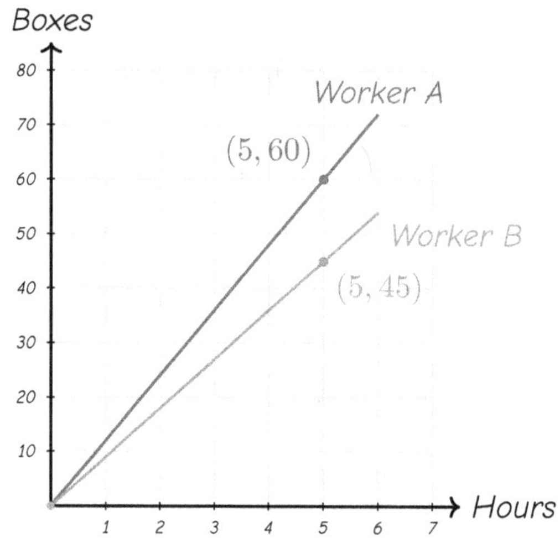

(A) *Worker A, by 3 boxes/hr*

(B) *Worker B, by 3 boxes/hr*

(C) *Worker A, by 15 boxes/hr*

(D) *They work at the same rate*

4. *A store has 300 items in stock. If 60% are on sale, how many items are on sale?*

(A) 120

(B) 150

(C) 180

(D) 200

Find more at
ViewMath.com/KS-Grade7

5. The diagram shows how a salesperson's earnings are calculated. What are the total earnings?

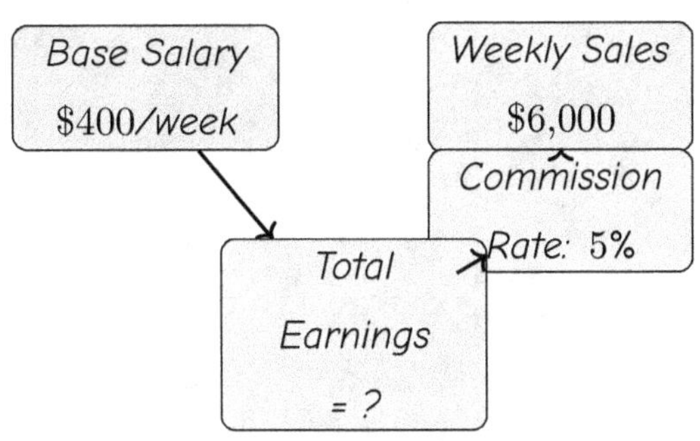

(A) $430

(B) $700

(C) $6,400

(D) $6,700

6. A jogger estimated running 5 miles but actually ran 4.8 miles. What is the percent error (rounded to the nearest tenth)?

Your Answer:

7. The number line below shows two points. Which statement is correct?

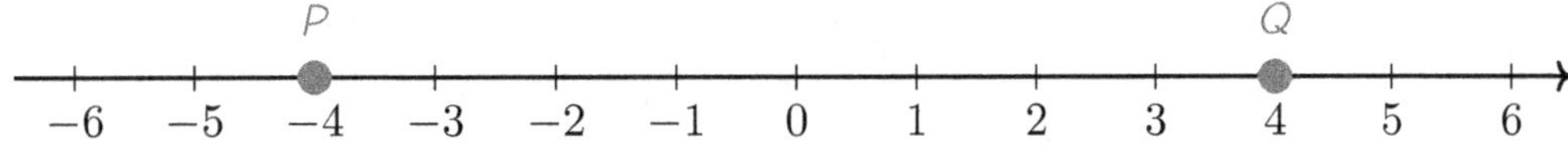

(A) P and Q are the same number

(B) P and Q are opposites

(C) $|P| > |Q|$

(D) $P > Q$

8. What is $0 + (-7)$?

(A) 7

(B) 0

(C) -7

(D) -14

Find more at
ViewMath.com/KS-Grade7

9. Evaluate $\frac{x^2-1}{4}$ when $x = 5$.

Your Answer:

10. Simplify $\frac{1}{2}x + \frac{3}{4}x - 2$.

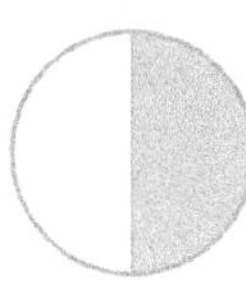

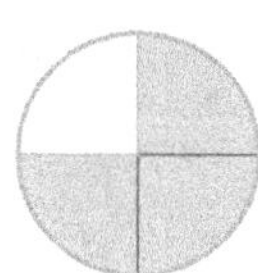

Your Answer:

11. The diagram shows a triangle with a perimeter of 39 cm. What is the value of x?

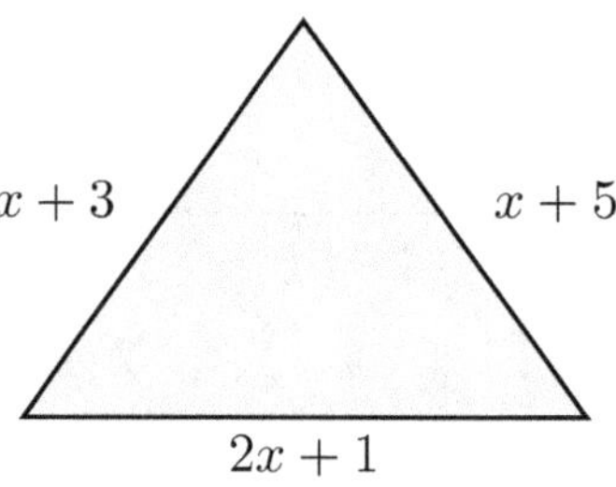

(A) $x = 7.5$

(B) $x = 10$

(C) $x = 6$

(D) $x = 8$

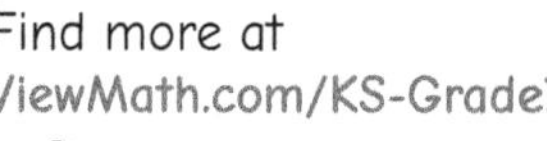

12. Four friends go to a museum. Each person pays for a ticket and a $3 audio guide. The total for all four people is $68. The equation $4(t+3) = 68$ represents this situation, where t is the ticket price. Use the model below to find t.

4 people

t	$3
t	$3
t	$3
t	$3

$\}$ $68

Your Answer:

13. A store marks down a jacket by $\frac{1}{4}$ of its original price p, then subtracts an additional $8. The sale price is $37. Find the original price.

Your Answer

14. Solve $2x + 3 > 11$.

(A) $x > 4$

(B) $x > 7$

(C) $x < 4$

(D) $x > 14$

15. What inequality is shown by a closed circle at -6 with shading to the right?

Your Answer:

Get Online

Find more at
ViewMath.com/KS-Grade7

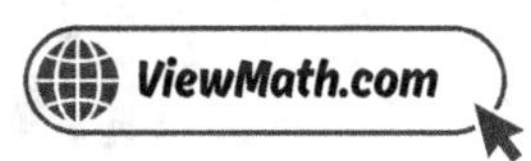

16. A drawing uses $1\ cm = 3\ m$. It is redrawn at $1\ cm = 9\ m$. A room that is $12\ cm$ on the original becomes how long?

(A) 4 cm

(B) 12 cm

(C) 36 cm

(D) 108 cm

17. Two sides of a triangle are 5 cm and 5 cm with an included angle of 60°. What type of triangle is formed?

Your Answer:

18. What condition (SSS, SAS, ASA, AAS, or AAA) gives infinitely many triangles?

Your Answer:

19. You cut a rectangular prism with a cut that passes through exactly three faces. What is the cross-section shape?

(A) Rectangle

(B) Triangle

(C) Pentagon

(D) Hexagon

20. A circle has a diameter of 14 cm. What is its area? Use $\pi \approx \frac{22}{7}$.

(A) $44\ cm^2$

(B) $154\ cm^2$

(C) $308\ cm^2$

(D) $616\ cm^2$

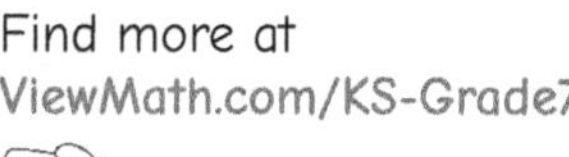

Find more at
ViewMath.com/KS-Grade7

21. A figure is made of a rectangle 12 cm by 5 cm with a right triangle removed. The triangle has legs 4 cm and 5 cm. What is the area of the remaining figure?

(A) 40 cm²

(B) 50 cm²

(C) 60 cm²

(D) 70 cm²

22. A triangular prism has a triangular base with base 6 cm and height 4 cm, and the prism is 10 cm long. The three rectangular faces have widths 6 cm, 5 cm, and 5 cm. What is the total surface area?

(A) 184 cm²

(B) 160 cm²

(C) 124 cm²

(D) 120 cm²

23. A rectangular fish tank is 50 cm long, 30 cm wide, and 40 cm tall. What is the volume?

(A) 120 cm³

(B) 6,000 cm³

(C) 60,000 cm³

(D) 600 cm³

24. In a school of 600 students, a random sample of 60 found that 15 students walk to school. Predict how many students in the entire school walk to school.

(A) 100

(B) 150

(C) 200

(D) 250

25. Which measure of variability is shown directly on a box plot?

(A) Mean absolute deviation (MAD)

(B) Standard deviation

(C) Interquartile range (IQR)

(D) Mean

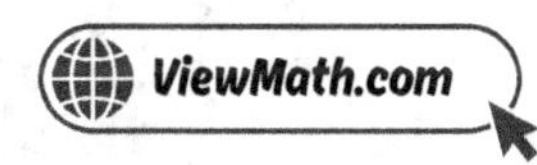

26. The table compares two delivery companies' shipping times (in days).

	Company X	Company Y
Mean	3.5 days	3.2 days
Median	3 days	3 days
Range	4 days	8 days
IQR	1.5 days	4 days

A customer wants the most reliable delivery time. Which company should they choose?

(A) Company Y, because its mean is lower

(B) Company X, because its IQR and range are both smaller

(C) Company Y, because its range includes more possibilities

(D) They are equally reliable

27. A jar has 5 green, 3 yellow, and 2 orange gumballs. What is the probability of NOT picking a green gumball?

(A) 0.5

(B) 0.3

(C) 0.7

(D) 0.2

28. A probability model has outcomes X, Y, and Z. $P(X) = 0.15$ and $P(Y) = 0.45$. What is $P(Z)$?

Your Answer:

29. A spinner has 4 equal sections $(1, 2, 3, 4)$ and a die is rolled. What is the probability that both show a 3?

(A) $\frac{1}{10}$

(B) $\frac{1}{24}$

(C) $\frac{2}{10}$

(D) $\frac{1}{4}$

30. A spinner has a 60% chance of landing on blue. In a simulation of 80 spins, how many times would you expect blue to appear?

Your Answer:

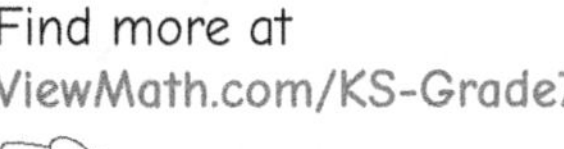
Find more at
ViewMath.com/KS-Grade7

 # ⭐ End of Practice Test 1 ⭐ 

Great job finishing the test!

 My Score

I got _____________ out of 30 questions right.

*Check your answers in the **Answer Key** at the back of the book.*

💡 *Review any questions you missed. That's how we learn!*

📊 Check Your Score Online!

*Visit **ViewMath Academy** to enter your answers and see which topics you need to review. You can also explore lessons, take quizzes, track your scores, and save your progress!*

viewmath.com/score/7.1.KS.16

Or go to viewmath.com/score and enter code: 7.1.KS.16

Practice Test 2

 *30 Questions*

✏️ Before You Start ✏️

- ✔ **Read each question carefully** before choosing your answer.
- ✔ **Show your work** on scratch paper when you need to.
- ✔ **Skip hard questions** and come back to them later.
- ✔ **Check your answers** when you're done.
- ✔ **Take your time** — there's no rush!

 You've Got This! 

Do your best and show what you know!

1. The table below shows a proportional relationship between gallons of gas and miles driven. What is k and what does it mean?

Gallons (x)	Miles (y)
2	54
5	135
8	216

(A) $k = 2$; uses 2 gallons per trip

(B) $k = 27$; drives 27 miles per gallon

(C) $k = 54$; drives 54 miles on 2 gallons

(D) $k = 135$; drives 135 miles on 5 gallons

2. The graph below shows the number of birdhouses a carpenter can build over time. What is the unit rate, and how many birdhouses can be built in 10 hours?

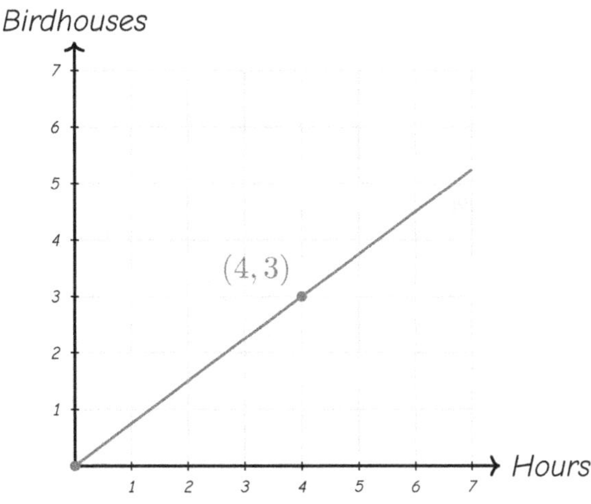

Your Answer:

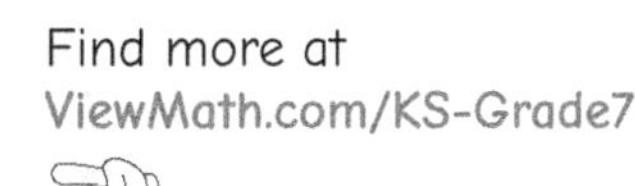

Find more at
ViewMath.com/KS-Grade7

3. The table shows how many batches of muffins a bakery can make and the total flour used. How many cups of flour are needed for 15 batches?

Batches	Flour (cups)
3	$7\frac{1}{2}$
6	15
9	$22\frac{1}{2}$
15	?

Your Answer:

4. A class has 32 students. If 75% passed the test, how many students passed?

(A) 20

(B) 24

(C) 25

(D) 28

5. A bill is \$86 and you leave a \$17.20 tip. What percent tip is that?

(A) 15%

(B) 17%

(C) 18%

(D) 20%

6. Two students estimated the number of beans in a jar. The actual count was 200. Student A guessed 180; Student B guessed 220. Who had the greater percent error?

(A) Student A

(B) Student B

(C) Same percent error

(D) Cannot be determined

Find more at
ViewMath.com/KS-Grade7

7. What is $|-9|$?

(A) -9

(B) 0

(C) $\frac{1}{9}$

(D) 9

8. Find the sum: $5 + (-11) + 3 + (-2)$.

Your Answer:

9. What is the value of $\frac{x}{2} - 4$ when $x = 10$?

(A) 3

(B) -1

(C) 1

(D) 9

10. Simplify $-2a + 5b + 7a - 3b$.

Your Answer:

11. Solve $8 = \frac{x}{3} + 2$.

(A) $x = 30$

(B) $x = 18$

(C) $x = 2$

(D) $x = 6$

12. Solve $2(x + 7) = -6$.

Your Answer:

Get Online

Find more at
ViewMath.com/KS-Grade7

ViewMath.com

13. A number line shows a point at x. The equation $\frac{x}{4} + 1.5 = 5$ tells you how to find x. Solve and identify where x is on the number line.

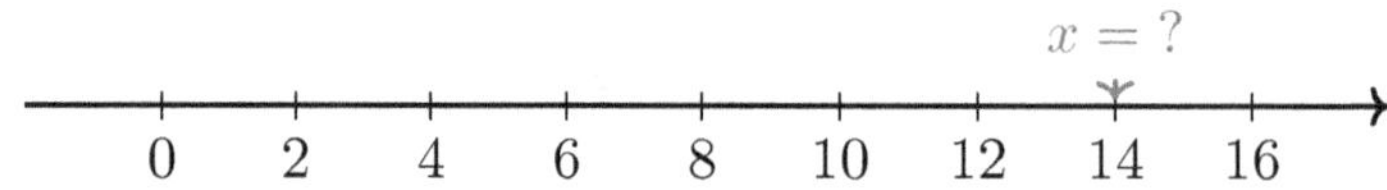

Your Answer

14. Solve $\frac{x}{2} + 7 \leq 12$.

Your Answer

15. Which inequality is shown by a closed circle at 7 with shading to the left?

(A) $x > 7$

(B) $x < 7$

(C) $x \geq 7$

(D) $x \leq 7$

16. A map uses $1\ cm = 20\ km$. You redraw it at $1\ cm = 10\ km$. What happens to the drawing?

(A) Every length is halved

(B) Every length stays the same

(C) Every length is doubled

(D) Every length is multiplied by 10

17. You know all three angles of a triangle: 50°, 60°, and 70°. How many triangles can be drawn?

(A) None

(B) Exactly one

(C) Exactly three

(D) More than one (infinitely many)

18. Can a triangle be formed with sides 7, 10, and 15?

(A) No, the triangle inequality fails

(B) Yes, exactly one triangle

(C) Yes, more than one triangle

(D) Yes, but only a right triangle

19. A rectangular prism has a base of 6 cm by 4 cm and a height of 10 cm. It is sliced parallel to the base. What are the dimensions of the cross-section?

Your Answer:

20. A circle has an area of 78.5 cm². Using $\pi \approx 3.14$, what is the radius?

(A) 4 cm

(B) 5 cm

(C) 10 cm

(D) 25 cm

21. A swimming pool is shaped like a rectangle 25 m by 10 m with a semicircle of diameter 10 m at one end. What is the total area? Use $\pi \approx 3.14$.

(A) 250 m^2

(B) 289.25 m^2

(C) 328.5 m^2

(D) 367.75 m^2

22. A triangular prism has a right-triangle base with legs 3 cm and 4 cm. The prism is 12 cm long. The hypotenuse of the triangle is 5 cm. What is the total surface area?

Your Answer:

Find more at
ViewMath.com/KS-Grade7

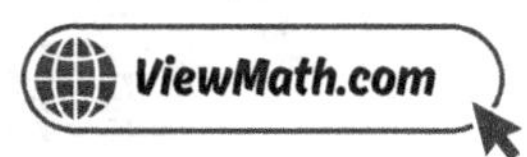

23. A triangular prism has a base that is a triangle with base 8 cm and height 3 cm. The prism is 10 cm long. What is the volume?

(A) $24\ cm^3$

(B) $80\ cm^3$

(C) $120\ cm^3$

(D) $240\ cm^3$

24. A factory produces 10,000 batteries per day. A sample of 200 batteries is tested, and 8 are defective. What percent of the sample is defective?

Your Answer:

25. The dot plots below show the number of push-ups completed by students in two gym classes.

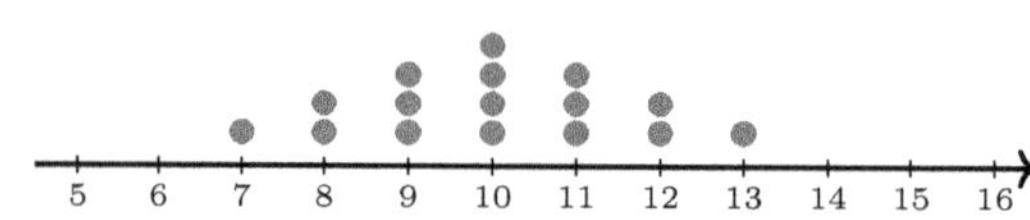

Which class has a higher center, and by approximately how many push-ups?

(A) Class 1, by about 3

(B) Class 2, by about 3

(C) Class 2, by about 6

(D) They have the same center

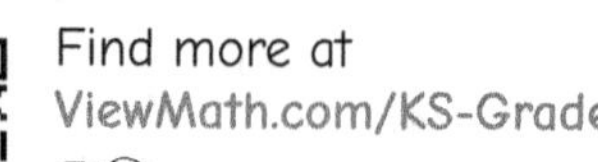

Find more at
ViewMath.com/KS-Grade7

26. *The dot plots show daily high temperatures (°F) for two cities over 10 days.*

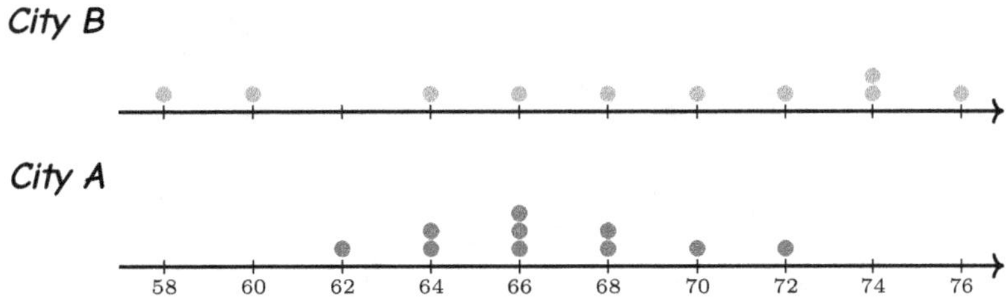

Find the mean and range for each city. Which city has more consistent temperatures?

Your Answer:

27. *What does a probability of 0 mean?*

(A) *The event is certain to happen*

(B) *The event is very likely to happen*

(C) *The event is impossible*

(D) *The event has a 50% chance of happening*

28. *A student creates a probability model for a spinner.* $P(red) = 0.25$, $P(blue) = 0.25$, $P(green) = 0.25$, $P(yellow) = 0.25$. *After 200 spins, the results are: red = 55, blue = 48, green = 52, yellow = 45. Is the model a good fit?*

(A) *No, the model is completely wrong*

(B) *Yes, the observed frequencies are reasonably close to 50 each*

(C) *No, because the results are not exactly 50 each*

(D) *Yes, because 200 is divisible by 4*

29. The tree diagram shows the outcomes for flipping two coins. What is the probability of getting at least one tail?

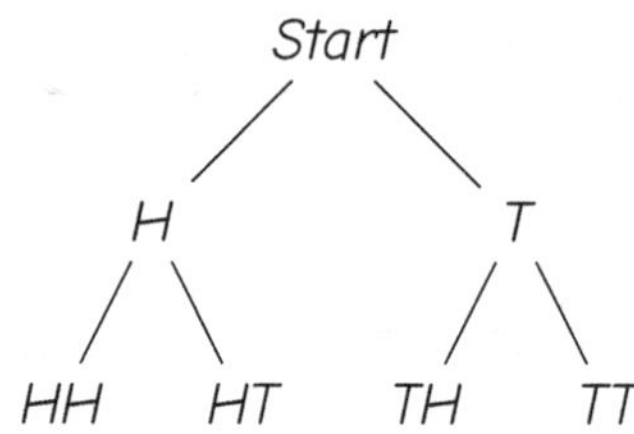

(A) $\frac{1}{4}$

(B) $\frac{1}{2}$

(C) $\frac{3}{4}$

(D) $\frac{2}{4}$

30. The bar graph shows the results of simulating a spinner 100 times. The spinner is supposed to land on each color with equal probability. Based on the simulation, does the spinner appear fair?

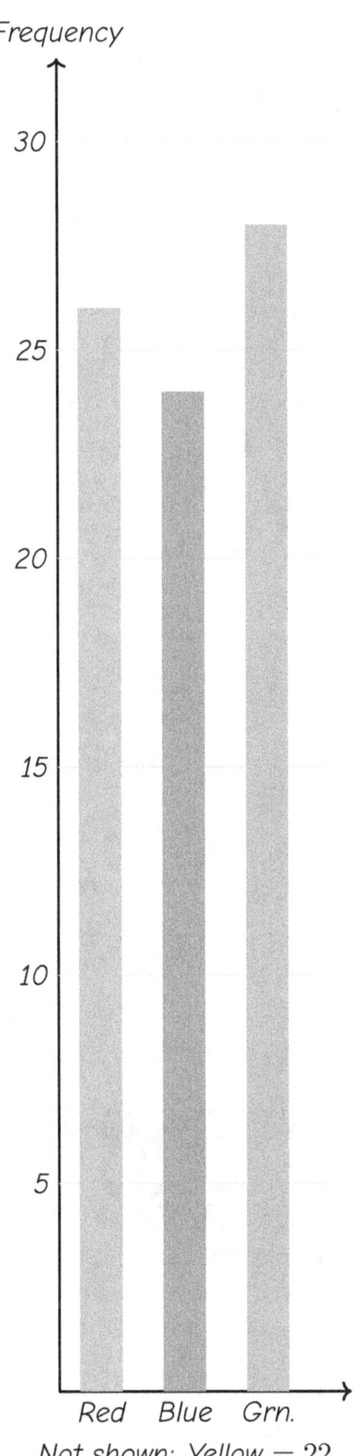

Not shown: Yellow $= 22$

(A) No, because the bars are different heights

(B) Yes, the frequencies $(26, 24, 28, 22)$ are all roughly close to 25

( ) Green is clearly the most likely color

(D) Cannot be determined from the graph

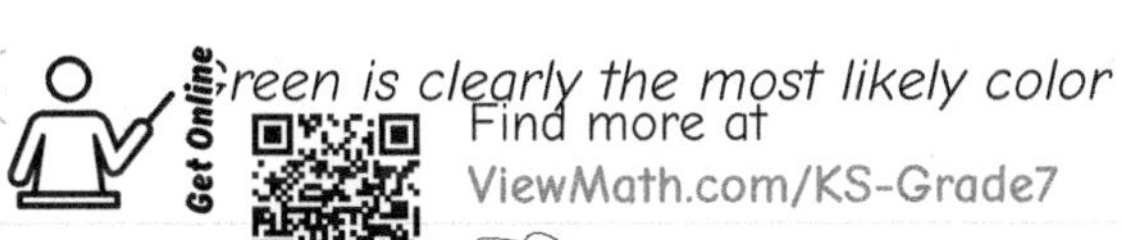

 End of Practice Test 2 

Great job finishing the test!

☑ My Score

I got __________ out of 30 questions right.

*Check your answers in the **Answer Key** at the back of the book.*

💡 *Review any questions you missed. That's how we learn!*

📊 Check Your Score Online!

Visit **ViewMath Academy** to enter your answers and see which topics you need to review. You can also explore lessons, take quizzes, track your scores, and save your progress!

viewmath.com/score/7.1.KS.17

Or go to viewmath.com/score and enter code: 7.1.KS.17

3

Practice Test 3

 30 Questions

---

✏️ Before You Start ✏️

- ✓ **Read each question carefully** before choosing your answer.
- ✓ **Show your work** on scratch paper when you need to.
- ✓ **Skip hard questions** and come back to them later.
- ✓ **Check your answers** when you're done.
- ✓ **Take your time** — there's no rush!

 ⭐ You've Got This! ⭐

Do your best and show what you know!

1. *A proportional table has $k = \frac{3}{4}$. Which pair could be in the table?*

  (A) $(8, 10)$ (B) $(8, 6)$

  (C) $(12, 8)$ (D) $(4, 2)$

2. *Two proportional lines are graphed. Line A is steeper than Line B. What does this tell you?*

  (A) Line A has a smaller unit rate   (B) Line A has a greater unit rate

  (C) Line B covers more distance   (D) Both lines have the same rate

3. *Store A sells 3 notebooks for \$7.50. Store B sells 5 notebooks for \$11.25. Which store offers the better deal?*

  (A) Store A at \$2.50 each   (B) Store B at \$2.25 each

  (C) Store A at \$2.25 each   (D) They cost the same

4. *63 is 90% of what number?*

  (A) 56.7   (B) 67

  (C) 70   (D) 72

5. *Estimate a 15% tip on a \$78 bill using the 10% method.*

  (A) About \$7.80   (B) About \$10.40

  (C) About \$11.70   (D) About \$15.60

6. *A student measured a table as 4.5 feet long. The actual length is 5 feet. What is the percent error?*

  (A) 0.5%   (B) 5%

  (C) 10%   (D) 11.1%

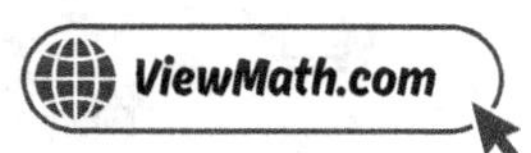

7. *For which value of n is $|n| = 10$?*

   (A) *Only* $n = 10$ (B) *Only* $n = -10$

   (C) $n = 10$ *or* $n = -10$ (D) $n = 0$

8. *What is $15 + (-15)$?*

   (A) 30   (B) -30

   (C) 15   (D) 0

9. *What is the value of $x^2 + 3x$ when $x = -2$?*

   (A) 10   (B) -2

   (C) -10 (D) 2

10. *Simplify $-6y + 4y - y$.*

   (A) $-3y$ (B) $-y$

   (C) $3y$ (D) $-11y$

11. *Solve $9 + 3x = 30$.*

   (A) $x = 13$ (B) $x = 3$

   (C) $x = 7$ (D) $x = 10$

12. *Solve $9(x - 3) = 45$.*

Your Answer:

Find more at
ViewMath.com/KS-Grade7

ViewMath.com

13. *Solve $-0.4y + 2 = 6$.*

   (A) $y = 10$

   (B) $y = -10$

   (C) $y = 20$

   (D) $y = -20$

14. *Solve $-5n + 10 \leq -15$.*

   Your Answer

15. *Solve $-3x + 12 \geq 0$ and describe the graph.*

   (A) Closed circle at 4, shade right

   (B) Open circle at 4, shade left

   (C) Closed circle at 4, shade left

   (D) Closed circle at -4, shade right

16. *A map uses 1 cm = 60 km. You redraw it at 1 cm = 20 km. A triangle on the original has an area of 4 cm^2. What is its area on the new map?*

   (A) 12 cm^2

   (B) 16 cm^2

   (C) 36 cm^2

   (D) 48 cm^2

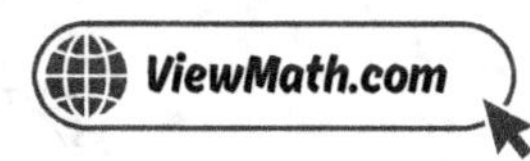

17. The diagram shows a triangle with the given measurements. How many different triangles can be drawn with these exact conditions?

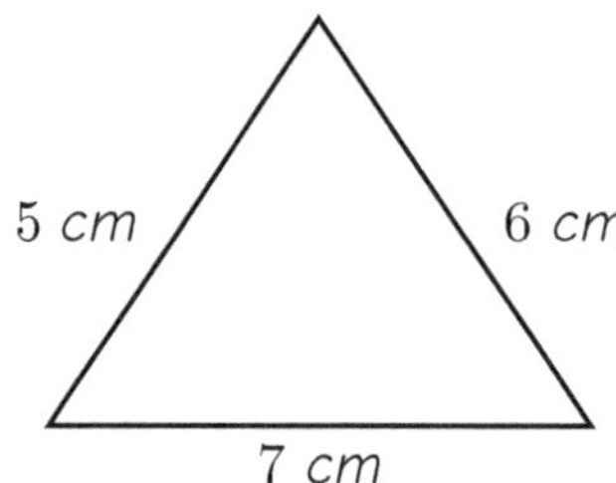

(A) None

(B) Exactly one

(C) Exactly two

(D) Infinitely many

18. A triangle has angles 90°, 45°, and 45°. Which statement is true?

(A) Exactly one such triangle exists

(B) Many triangles with these angles exist, in different sizes

(C) No such triangle exists because two angles are equal

(D) No such triangle exists because the angles don't sum to 180°

19. A triangular prism is sliced with a vertical cut perpendicular to the triangular bases. What shape is the cross-section?

(A) Triangle

(B) Rectangle

(C) Circle

(D) Trapezoid

20. A circular rug has a diameter of 8 feet. What is the area of the rug? Use $\pi \approx 3.14$.

(A) $25.12 \ ft^2$

(B) $50.24 \ ft^2$

(C) $200.96 \ ft^2$

(D) $64 \ ft^2$

Find more at
ViewMath.com/KS-Grade7

21. A figure is made of a right triangle with legs 6 cm and 8 cm, and a rectangle 8 cm by 3 cm. What is the total area?

(A) 24 cm^2 (B) 48 cm^2

(C) 36 cm^2 (D) 72 cm^2

22. The net shown below folds into a rectangular prism. Find the total surface area.

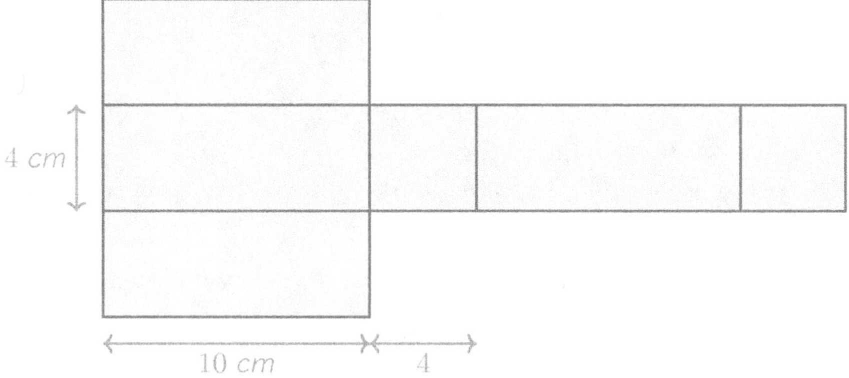

Your Answer:

23. A trapezoidal prism has a trapezoidal base with parallel sides 4 cm and 6 cm, height 3 cm, and the prism length is 10 cm. What is its volume?

(A) 60 cm^3 (B) 120 cm^3

(C) 150 cm^3 (D) 180 cm^3

24. Which of the following increases the reliability of conclusions drawn from a sample?

(A) Using a smaller sample   (B) Using a larger random sample

(C) Surveying only people who agree with you   (D) Using a non-random sample

25. *School A: median score 88, MAD 4. School B: median score 82, MAD 4. The difference in medians expressed in MADs is:*

(A) 1 MAD

(B) 1.5 MADs

(C) 2 MADs

(D) 4 MADs

26. *Group X: mean 45, MAD 6. Group Y: mean 57, MAD 6. Express the difference in means as a multiple of MAD.*

Your Answer

27. *Jasmine says the probability of picking a vowel from the letters of the word MATH is $\frac{2}{4}$. Is she correct?*

(A) Yes, because there are 2 vowels in MATH

(B) No, there is only 1 vowel in MATH, so the probability is $\frac{1}{4}$

(C) No, the probability is $\frac{3}{4}$

(D) Yes, because half of all letters are vowels

28. *A bag contains 4 red marbles and 1 blue marble. Which type of probability model does this represent?*

(A) Uniform

(B) Non-uniform

(C) Both uniform and non-uniform

(D) Neither

29. *Two dice are rolled. What is the probability of getting a sum of 2?*

(A) $\frac{1}{6}$

(B) $\frac{1}{12}$

(C) $\frac{1}{36}$

(D) $\frac{2}{36}$

Find more at
ViewMath.com/KS-Grade7

30. *You simulate flipping a coin 3 times and counting how many times all 3 are heads. In 40 simulations, all 3 heads occurs 6 times. What is the experimental probability?*

(A) $\frac{6}{40} = 0.15$

(B) $\frac{1}{8} = 0.125$

(C) $\frac{3}{40} = 0.075$

(D) $\frac{6}{120} = 0.05$

⭐ *End of Practice Test 3* ⭐

Great job finishing the test!

 **My Score**

I got __________ out of 30 questions right.

*Check your answers in the **Answer Key** at the back of the book.*

💡 *Review any questions you missed. That's how we learn!*

📊 **Check Your Score Online!**

*Visit **ViewMath Academy** to enter your answers and see which topics you need to review. You can also explore lessons, take quizzes, track your scores, and save your progress!*

viewmath.com/score/7.1.KS.18

Or go to viewmath.com/score and enter code: 7.1.KS.18

Practice Test 4

✅ 30 Questions

✏️ Before You Start ✏️

- ✔ **Read each question carefully** before choosing your answer.
- ✔ **Show your work** on scratch paper when you need to.
- ✔ **Skip hard questions** and come back to them later.
- ✔ **Check your answers** when you're done.
- ✔ **Take your time** — there's no rush!

⭐ *You've Got This!* ⭐

Do your best and show what you know!

1. *What is the constant of proportionality (k) for the table below?*

x	y
3	12
5	20
8	32

(A) 3

(B) 4

(C) 8

(D) 12

2. *A proportional graph shows total cost versus hours of tutoring. The point $(3, 67.50)$ is on the graph. How much does 5 hours of tutoring cost?*

Your Answer:

3. *A factory produces 168 items in 7 hours. Another factory produces 200 items in 8 hours. Which factory is more productive?*

(A) Factory 1, at 24 items/hr

(B) Factory 2, at 25 items/hr

(C) They produce the same rate

(D) Factory 1, at 25 items/hr

4. *A jar has 250 candies. If 44% are chocolate, how many chocolate candies are there?*

Your Answer:

5. *A restaurant bill is $40. You leave a 15% tip. How much is the tip?*

(A) $4.00

(B) $5.00

(C) $6.00

(D) $8.00

Find more at
ViewMath.com/KS-Grade7

6. In the percent error formula, why do we use absolute value?

(A) To make the calculation easier

(B) Because the answer must be positive

(C) Because we only care about the size of the error, not the direction

(D) To convert the answer to a percent

7. Which statement about absolute value is FALSE?

(A) $|-5| = 5$

(B) $|0| = 0$

(C) Absolute value can be negative

(D) $|3| = |-3|$

8. A hiker starts at an elevation of -30 feet (below sea level). She climbs 45 feet. What is her new elevation?

Your Answer

9. Which expression represents "the product of 7 and a number p, decreased by 12"?

(A) $7(p - 12)$

(B) $12 - 7p$

(C) $7p - 12$

(D) $7 + p - 12$

10. Simplify $7x + 3x$.

(A) $10x$

(B) $21x$

(C) $10x^2$

(D) $73x$

11. Solve $\dfrac{w}{5} + 12 = 20$.

(A) $w = 40$

(B) $w = 160$

(C) $w = 8$

(D) $w = 1.6$

12. *Solve* $5(2x - 3) = 35$.

Your Answer:

13. *Use the fraction bar model to solve:* $\frac{2}{3}x = 8$. *What is* x?

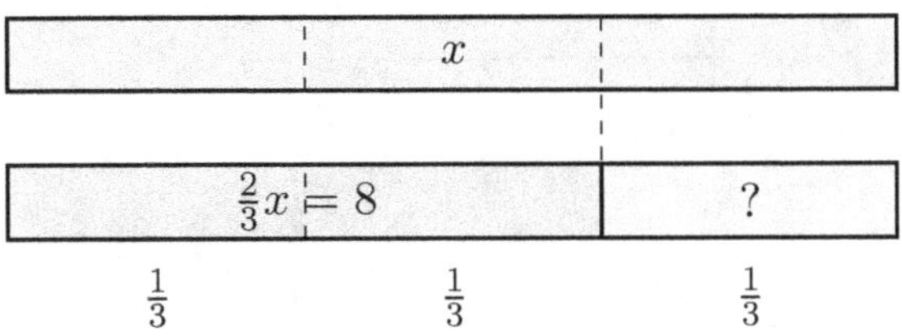

A) $x = 12$

B) $x = 16$

C) $x = 10$

D) $x = 5\frac{1}{3}$

14. *Solve* $8 - 3x \geq 23$.

Your Answer:

15. *Solve* $-2x \leq 10$ *and describe the graph.*

A) *Closed circle at* -5*, shade left*

B) *Closed circle at* 5*, shade left*

C) *Closed circle at* -5*, shade right*

D) *Open circle at* -5*, shade right*

16. A triangle on Drawing A (scale 1 cm = 4 m) has the dimensions shown below. Drawing B uses scale 1 cm = 2 m. What is the base of the triangle on Drawing B?

Drawing A

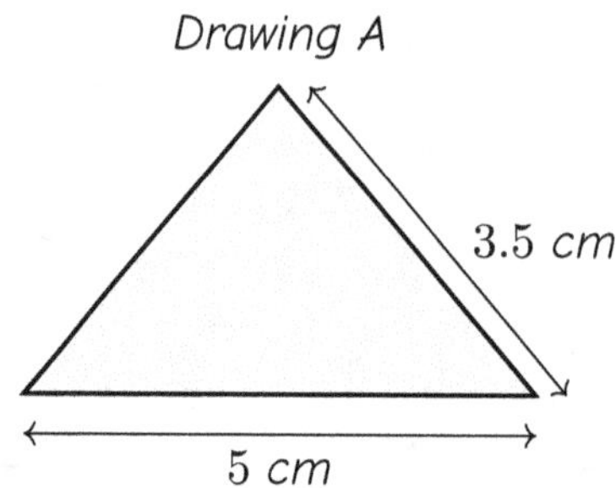

(A) 2.5 cm

(B) 5 cm

(C) 10 cm

(D) 20 cm

17. Marcus wants to draw a triangle with angles 60°, 60°, and 60° and a side of 4 cm. How many different triangles can he draw?

(A) None

(B) Exactly one

(C) Exactly three

(D) Infinitely many

18. Can a triangle have angles 90°, 100°, and −10°?

(A) Yes, it is a right triangle

(B) Yes, because the sum is 180°

(C) No, because an angle cannot be negative

(D) No, because the sum is not 180°

19. Which cross-section is NOT possible from slicing a rectangular prism?

(A) Rectangle

(B) Triangle

(C) Circle

(D) Pentagon

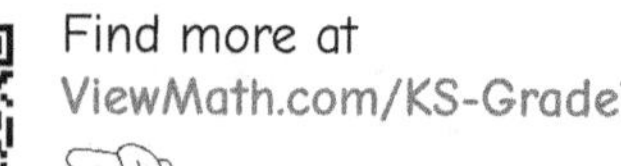
Find more at
ViewMath.com/KS-Grade7

20. *What is the area of a circle with a radius of 10 cm? Use $\pi \approx 3.14$.*

(A) $31.4\ cm^2$ (B) $62.8\ cm^2$

(C) $100\ cm^2$ (D) $314\ cm^2$

21. *A shape is made of a square with side 8 cm and a semicircle with diameter 8 cm attached to one side. What is the area? Use $\pi \approx 3.14$.*

(A) $64\ cm^2$ (B) $89.12\ cm^2$

(C) $114.24\ cm^2$ (D) $139.12\ cm^2$

22. *A rectangular prism has dimensions 7 m by 4 m by 3 m. What is the area of the largest face?*

(A) $12\ m^2$ (B) $21\ m^2$

(C) $28\ m^2$ (D) $84\ m^2$

23. *The figure shows unit cubes stacked into an L-shape. Each cube has a side length of 1 cm. What is the total volume?*

(A) $8\ cm^3$ (B) $11\ cm^3$

(C) $15\ cm^3$ (D) $33\ cm^3$

24. *Give one reason why a sample might not perfectly represent a population.*

Your Answer:

Find more at
ViewMath.com/KS-Grade7

25. When comparing two populations visually, you should look at:

(A) Only the center (mean or median)

(B) Only the spread (range or MAD)

(C) Both the center and the spread

(D) Only the largest and smallest values

26. Store A daily sales: mean $500, MAD $40. Store B daily sales: mean $620, MAD $40. The difference in means in MADs is:

(A) 1.5 MADs

(B) 3 MADs

(C) 40 MADs

(D) 120 MADs

27. Marcus says the probability of his basketball team winning tonight is $\frac{3}{4}$. Which statement best describes this?

(A) The team will definitely win

(B) The team is unlikely to win

(C) The team is likely to win, but not certain

(D) The team has an equal chance of winning or losing

28. A coin is weighted so that heads comes up 60% of the time. What is the probability of tails?

(A) 0.60

(B) 0.50

(C) 0.40

(D) 0.30

Find more at
ViewMath.com/KS-Grade7

29. Look at the tree diagram for flipping three coins. What is the probability of getting exactly 2 tails? Write your answer as a fraction in simplest form.

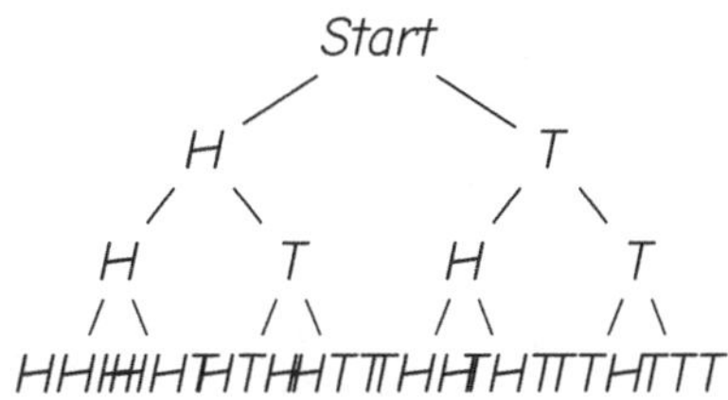

Your Answer:

30. A student wants to simulate the probability that exactly 2 out of 3 students pass a test, where each student has a 50% chance. Which model would work?

(A) Roll one die: odd = pass, even = fail

(B) Flip 3 coins: heads = pass, tails = fail; count exactly 2 heads

(C) Draw 3 marbles from a bag of 2 red and 1 blue

(D) Flip 1 coin 3 times and count all tails

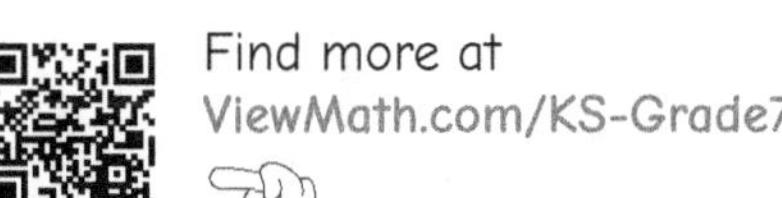

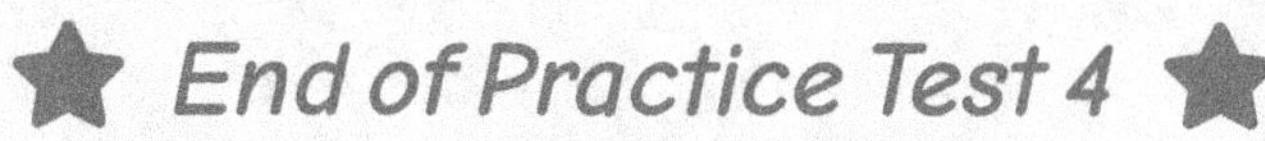 End of Practice Test 4

Great job finishing the test!

My Score

I got _____________ out of 30 questions right.

*Check your answers in the **Answer Key** at the back of the book.*

Review any questions you missed. That's how we learn!

Check Your Score Online!

*Visit **ViewMath Academy** to enter your answers and see which topics you need to review. You can also explore lessons, take quizzes, track your scores, and save your progress!*

viewmath.com/score/7.1.KS.19

Or go to viewmath.com/score and enter code: 7.1.KS.19

Practice Test 5

 *30 Questions*

✏️ Before You Start ✏️

- ✔ **Read each question carefully** before choosing your answer.
- ✔ **Show your work** on scratch paper when you need to.
- ✔ **Skip hard questions** and come back to them later.
- ✔ **Check your answers** when you're done.
- ✔ **Take your time** — there's no rush!

 **You've Got This!** 

Do your best and show what you know!

1. A factory produces widgets at a constant rate. In $2\frac{1}{2}$ hours it makes 175 widgets. What is k in widgets per hour?

Your Answer

2. A proportional graph passes through $(3, 18)$. What is the unit rate?

(A) 3

(B) 6

(C) 15

(D) 18

3. A 12-oz box of cereal costs \$3.60. A 20-oz box costs \$5.40. Which is the better value?

(A) 12-oz box at \$0.30/oz

(B) 20-oz box at \$0.27/oz

(C) 12-oz box at \$0.27/oz

(D) They are the same price per ounce

4. The tape diagram below represents a whole quantity. What percent of the total is the shaded portion?

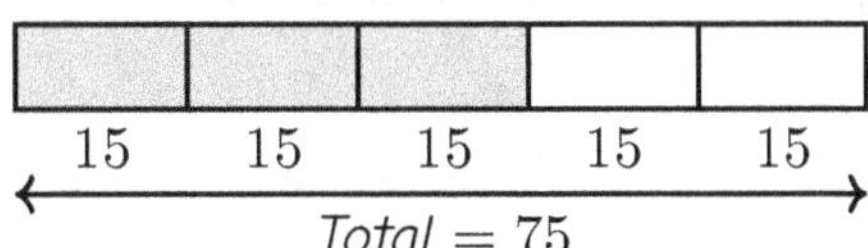

(A) 40%

(B) 45%

(C) 50%

(D) 60%

5. A real estate agent earns 3% commission on a \$250,000 home sale. What does she earn?

(A) \$750

(B) \$2,500

(C) \$7,500

(D) \$75,000

6. An architect estimated a building would be 45 meters tall. The actual height is 42 meters. What is the percent error (rounded to the nearest tenth)?

Your Answer:

7. Which statement is true?

(A) $-5 > -2$

(B) $-3 > 0$

(C) $-7 < -4$

(D) $0 < -1$

8. What value of n makes $(-9) + n = -2$ true?

(A) -11

(B) -7

(C) 7

(D) 11

9. Which expression means "half the sum of a number k and 10"?

(A) $\frac{k}{2} + 10$

(B) $\frac{k+10}{2}$

(C) $\frac{10k}{2}$

(D) $\frac{k}{2+10}$

10. The perimeter of a triangle is $3x + 2 + 5x - 1 + 2x + 4$. Write the simplified expression for the perimeter.

Your Answer:

11. Solve $2x + 15 = 31$.

Your Answer:

Find more at
ViewMath.com/KS-Grade7

ViewMath.com

12. Solve $-4(y + 3) = 28$.

(A) $y = 4$

(B) $y = -10$

(C) $y = 10$

(D) $y = -4$

13. Solve $-0.3x + 4.2 = 1.8$.

Your Answer:

14. A movie theater requires you to be more than 48 inches tall for a ride. You are 42 inches tall and grow g inches per year. Which inequality finds how many years until you are tall enough?

(A) $42 + g > 48$

(B) $42g > 48$

(C) $48 - g > 42$

(D) $42 - g > 48$

15. The graph of an inequality has an open circle at -1 and is shaded to the left. Which inequality matches?

(A) $x \leq -1$

(B) $x < -1$

(C) $x \geq -1$

(D) $x > -1$

16. A blueprint uses scale $1 : 80$. You redraw at scale $1 : 20$. A room is 2 cm by 3 cm on the original. What is the area of the room on the new drawing?

Your Answer:

17. A parallelogram has side lengths 5 cm and 8 cm. How many different parallelograms can be drawn?

(A) None

(B) Exactly one

(C) Exactly two

(D) More than one

Find more at
ViewMath.com/KS-Grade7

18. Can a triangle have angles 50°, 60°, and 80°?

(A) Yes, because the angles are all positive

(B) Yes, because each angle is less than 180°

(C) No, because $50 + 60 + 80 = 190 \neq 180$

(D) No, because the angles are not equal

19. Which 3D figure always has circular cross-sections when cut parallel to its base?

(A) Rectangular prism

(B) Triangular pyramid

(C) Cone

(D) Cube

20. A sprinkler waters a circular area with a radius of 5 meters. How many square meters does it water? Use $\pi \approx 3.14$

(A) $31.4 \ m^2$

(B) $50 \ m^2$

(C) $78.5 \ m^2$

(D) $157 \ m^2$

21. An H-shaped figure is made of three rectangles. The top and bottom bars are each 10 cm by 2 cm. The middle vertical bar is 2 cm by 6 cm. What is the total area?

Your Answer:

22. How many faces does a rectangular prism have?

(A) 4

(B) 5

(C) 6

(D) 8

Find more at
ViewMath.com/KS-Grade7

ViewMath.com

23. A moving box is 2 ft long, 2 ft wide, and 3 ft tall. How many of these boxes can fit in a space that is 6 ft by 4 ft by 3 ft?

(A) 3

(B) 6

(C) 12

(D) 18

24. A school has 800 students. The principal surveys 50 students about their favorite subject. What is the population?

(A) The 50 surveyed students

(B) All 800 students in the school

(C) The principal

(D) The students who like math

25. Team A's scores: mean 72, MAD 3. Team B's scores: mean 74, MAD 8. Which team is more consistent?

(A) Team A because its MAD is smaller

(B) Team B because its mean is higher

(C) Team A because its mean is lower

(D) Team B because its MAD is larger

26. Two groups have the same mean but different MADs. What does this tell you?

(A) One group scored higher than the other

(B) The groups have different levels of variability

(C) The groups are identical

(D) The means were calculated incorrectly

27. The probability that an event will happen is $\frac{3}{8}$. What is the probability that the event will NOT happen? Write your answer as a fraction.

Your Answer:

28. A bag has tiles labeled A, A, A, B, B. What is the probability of drawing a B?

(A) $\frac{1}{5}$ (B) $\frac{2}{3}$

(C) $\frac{2}{5}$ (D) $\frac{3}{5}$

29. The table shows all possible products when two dice are rolled. How many outcomes give a product of 6? Write the probability as a fraction in simplest form.

×	1	2	3	4	5	6
1	1	2	3	4	5	6
2	2	4	6	8	10	12
3	3	6	9	12	15	18
4	4	8	12	16	20	24
5	5	10	15	20	25	30
6	6	12	18	24	30	36

Your Answer:

30. Which of the following is the FIRST step in designing a simulation?

(A) Record the results   (B) Run many trials

(C) Identify the event and its possible outcomes   (D) Calculate the experimental probability

Find more at
ViewMath.com/KS-Grade7

 # End of Practice Test 5 

Great job finishing the test!

☑ My Score

I got ___________ out of 30 questions right.

*Check your answers in the **Answer Key** at the back of the book.*

💡 *Review any questions you missed. That's how we learn!*

📊 Check Your Score Online!

Visit **ViewMath Academy** to enter your answers and see which topics you need to review. You can also explore lessons, take quizzes, track your scores, and save your progress!

viewmath.com/score/7.1.KS.20

Or go to viewmath.com/score and enter code: 7.1.KS.20

Practice Test 6

 30 Questions

 Before You Start 

- ✓ **Read each question carefully** before choosing your answer.
- ✓ **Show your work** on scratch paper when you need to.
- ✓ **Skip hard questions** and come back to them later.
- ✓ **Check your answers** when you're done.
- ✓ **Take your time** — there's no rush!

 You've Got This! 

Do your best and show what you know!

1. A proportional graph passes through $(6, 15)$. What is k?

Your Answer:

2. A proportional graph passes through $(4, 10)$. What is y when $x = 7$?

(A) 13

(B) 17

(C) 17.5

(D) 28

3. A car uses 3 gallons of gas every 87 miles. How many gallons does it need for a 435-mile trip?

(A) 10

(B) 12

(C) 15

(D) 18

4. 45 is 75% of what number?

(A) 33.75

(B) 50

(C) 56

(D) 60

5. An event planner charges a 10% planning fee plus a 3% coordination fee. If an event costs $4,000, what are the total fees?

(A) $120

(B) $400

(C) $520

(D) $1,300

Find more at
ViewMath.com/KS-Grade7

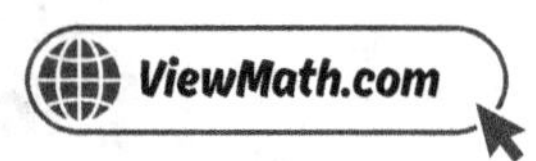

6. A scientist predicted a chemical reaction would produce 30 grams. It actually produced 28 grams. What is the percent error?

    (A) 2%   (B) 6.7%

    (C) 7.1%   (D) 14.3%

7. What is the opposite of the opposite of 4?

    (A) -4 (B) 0

    (C) 4   (D) $\frac{1}{4}$

8. Which pair of integers has a sum of -6?

    (A) 4 and -10 (B) -3 and -9

    (C) 8 and -2 (D) -1 and -4

9. Which expression means "a number n divided by 4, then increased by 3"?

    (A) $\frac{n+3}{4}$ (B) $\frac{4}{n} + 3$

    (C) $\frac{n}{4} + 3$ (D) $4n + 3$

10. Simplify $-4x + 9 + 7x - 3$.

    (A) $3x + 6$ (B) $-11x + 6$

    (C) $3x - 6$ (D) $11x + 12$

Find more at
ViewMath.com/KS-Grade7

11. Solve $50 - 4x = 18$.

(A) $x = -8$ (B) $x = 17$

(C) $x = 8$ (D) $x = 12$

12. The rectangle below has an area of 56 square cm. What is the value of x?

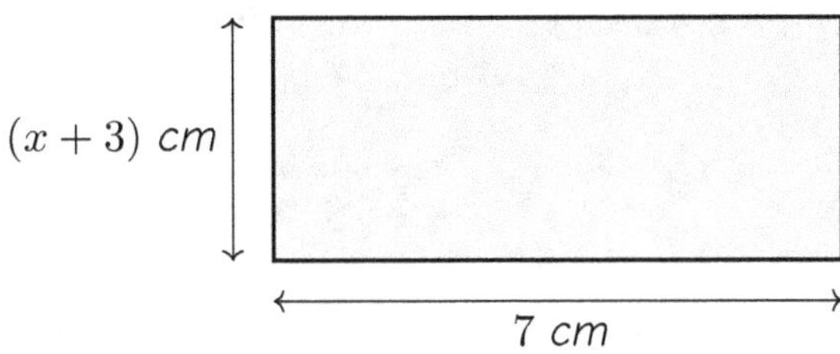

(A) $x = 5$ (B) $x = 8$

(C) $x = 11$ (D) $x = 4$

13. Solve $2.5x - 7.5 = 10$.

Your Answer

14. A student solved $-2x + 8 > 14$ and wrote $x > -3$. What error did the student make?

(A) Forgot to subtract 8   (B) Divided by 2 instead of -2

(C) Forgot to flip the inequality sign   (D) Added 8 instead of subtracting

15. Solve $5 - x > 8$ and describe the graph.

(A) Open circle at 3, shade right   (B) Open circle at -3, shade left

(C) Closed circle at -3, shade left   (D) Open circle at -3, shade right

16. A drawing uses $1\ cm = 6\ m$. It is redrawn at $1\ cm = 2\ m$. The original drawing is 8 cm by 5 cm. What is the perimeter of the new drawing?

(A) 26 cm

(B) 39 cm

(C) 78 cm

(D) 120 cm

17. A triangle has two sides of length 8 cm and 12 cm. What is the range of possible lengths for the third side?

Your Answer

18. You are given two sides (5 cm and 7 cm) and the included angle (90°). Is the resulting triangle unique? What type of triangle is it?

Your Answer

19. You slice a cube with a vertical cut from one face to the opposite face, perpendicular to the base. What is the most likely cross-section shape?

(A) Square or rectangle

(B) Circle

(C) Triangle

(D) Hexagon

20. A circle has an area of $12.56\ m^2$. Using $\pi \approx 3.14$, what is the diameter?

Your Answer

Find more at
ViewMath.com/KS-Grade7

21. A rectangular room is 14 ft by 10 ft. There is a built-in closet that is 3 ft by 4 ft. What is the area of the room not including the closet?

(A) 128 ft^2

(B) 140 ft^2

(C) 152 ft^2

(D) 12 ft^2

22. A cereal box is 25 cm tall, 18 cm wide, and 5 cm deep. How much cardboard is needed to make the box?

Your Answer:

23. A rectangular prism is 8 in by 5 in by 4 in. Another is 10 in by 4 in by 4 in. Which has more volume and .by how much?

(A) First prism, by 10 in^3

(B) Second prism, by 10 in^3

(C) First prism, by 20 in^3

(D) They have the same volume

24. A random sample means that:

(A) Only the best members are chosen

(B) The largest possible group is chosen

(C) Every member of the population has an equal chance of being selected

(D) Only volunteers are selected

25. When is a dot plot a better choice than a box plot for comparing two groups?

(A) When data sets are very large

(B) When you want to see every individual data point

(C) When you only want to compare medians

(D) When the data is categorical

Find more at
ViewMath.com/KS-Grade7

26. *Data set:* $12, 15, 18, 20, 22, 25, 28.$ *What is the median?*

(A) 18

(B) 20

(C) 22

(D) 19

27. *Which of these events is impossible?*

(A) Rolling a 5 on a standard die

(B) Flipping heads on a fair coin

(C) Drawing a green marble from a bag of only red and blue marbles

(D) Picking a number less than 10 from the numbers 1 to 20

28. *A spinner is divided into 4 sections with probabilities:* $red = 0.4,$ $blue = 0.3,$ $green = 0.2,$ $yellow = 0.1.$ *What type of model is this?*

(A) Uniform, because there are 4 sections

(B) Non-uniform, because the probabilities are different

(C) Invalid, because the probabilities don't add up to 1

(D) Uniform, because all sections are on the same spinner

29. *A coin is flipped and a die is rolled. What is the probability of getting tails and an even number?*

(A) $\frac{1}{12}$

(B) $\frac{1}{6}$

(C) $\frac{1}{4}$

(D) $\frac{1}{2}$

30. *What is a simulation?*

(A) A way to calculate exact probabilities

(B) A model that uses random numbers or objects to imitate a real event

(C) A method that always gives the same result

(D) A graph that shows all possible outcomes

Find more at
ViewMath.com/KS-Grade7

 End of Practice Test 6 

Great job finishing the test!

✅ My Score

I got _____________ out of 30 questions right.

Check your answers in the **Answer Key** at the back of the book.

💡 Review any questions you missed. That's how we learn!

📊 Check Your Score Online!

Visit **ViewMath Academy** to enter your answers and see which topics you need to review. You can also explore lessons, take quizzes, track your scores, and save your progress!

viewmath.com/score/7.1.KS.21

Or go to *viewmath.com/score* and enter code: 7.1.KS.21

Practice Test 7

 30 Questions

 Before You Start 

- ✓ **Read each question carefully** before choosing your answer.
- ✓ **Show your work** on scratch paper when you need to.
- ✓ **Skip hard questions** and come back to them later.
- ✓ **Check your answers** when you're done.
- ✓ **Take your time** — there's no rush!

 You've Got This! 

Do your best and show what you know!

1. Find the missing value in the proportional table.

x	y
5	20
9	?

Your Answer:

2. Which statement about proportional graphs is FALSE?

(A) They always pass through the origin

(B) The slope equals the unit rate

(C) A steeper line means a larger k

(D) The line can be curved

3. A cyclist rides 42 miles in 3 hours. At this rate, how long does it take to ride 98 miles?

Your Answer:

4. 9 is 12% of what number?

(A) 1.08

(B) 36

(C) 72

(D) 75

5. An online marketplace charges a 4% seller fee. A seller lists an item for $85. How much does the seller receive after the fee?

Your Answer:

6. You estimated there were 50 marbles in a jar. The actual count was 40. What is the percent error?

(A) 10%

(B) 20%

(C) 25%

(D) 50%

7. Which integer is 5 units to the left of 2 on the number line?

Your Answer

8. A diver is at -20 feet. She rises 8 feet. What is her new depth?

(A) -28 feet

(B) -12 feet

(C) 12 feet

(D) 28 feet

9. Which expression represents "6 more than twice a number n"?

(A) $6n + 2$

(B) $2n + 6$

(C) $2(n + 6)$

(D) $6 \times 2n$

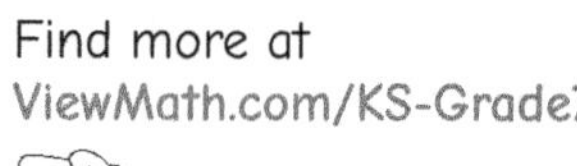
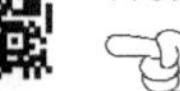

Find more at
ViewMath.com/KS-Grade7

ViewMath.com

10. *Simplify* $\frac{3}{4}n - \frac{1}{4}n + 5$.

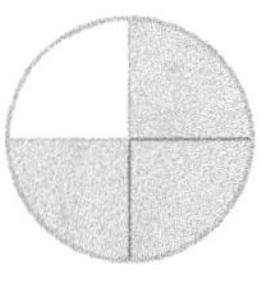

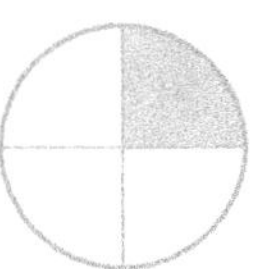

(A) $\frac{1}{2}n + 5$

(B) $n + 5$

(C) $\frac{3}{4}n + 5$

(D) $\frac{2}{4}n - 5$

11. *Solve* $100 - 7x = 37$.

Your Answer

12. *A student solved* $3(x+4) = 30$ *and wrote:* $3x + 4 = 30$, $3x = 26$, $x = \frac{26}{3}$. *What was the student's error?*

(A) Divided by 3 instead of subtracting

(B) Did not distribute 3 to the 4

(C) Subtracted 4 from the wrong side

(D) Forgot to check the answer

13. *A recipe calls for* $\frac{3}{4}$ *cup of sugar per batch. You already used* $\frac{1}{2}$ *cup. You have* $2\frac{3}{4}$ *cups total. The equation* $\frac{3}{4}b + \frac{1}{2} = 2\frac{3}{4}$ *finds how many more batches b you can make. What is b?*

(A) $b = 3$

(B) $b = 4$

(C) $b = 2$

(D) $b = 3\frac{2}{3}$

14. *Which inequality means "no more than 25"?*

(A) $x > 25$

(B) $x \geq 25$

(C) $x < 25$

(D) $x \leq 25$

15. *Solve $3x + 4 > 16$. Describe the graph on a number line.*

Your Answer:

16. *A blueprint uses 1 cm $= 4$ m. You want to redraw it at 1 cm $= 8$ m. A wall that is 10 cm on the original becomes how long on the new drawing?*

(A) 5 cm

(B) 10 cm

(C) 20 cm

(D) 40 cm

17. *Can you draw a triangle with sides 3 cm, 4 cm, and 8 cm?*

(A) Yes, and it is a unique triangle

(B) Yes, and more than one triangle is possible

(C) No, because the angles don't add to 180°

(D) No, because $3 + 4 < 8$

18. *Which set of measurements does NOT determine a unique triangle?*

(A) Sides 3, 4, 5

(B) Sides 7 and 9 with included angle 50°

(C) Angles 40°, 70°, 70°

(D) Angles 30°, 60° with included side 10 cm

19. *A cylinder is sliced with a vertical cut through its center, perpendicular to the base. What shape is the cross-section?*

(A) Circle

(B) Rectangle

(C) Oval

(D) Triangle

20. *Find the area of a semicircle with a diameter of 10 cm. Use $\pi \approx 3.14$.*

Your Answer:

21. *A T-shaped figure can be broken into a 12 cm by 2 cm horizontal rectangle and a 2 cm by 8 cm vertical rectangle. What is the total area?*

(A) $24\ cm^2$

(B) $32\ cm^2$

(C) $40\ cm^2$

(D) $48\ cm^2$

22. *What does surface area measure?*

(A) The space inside a 3D figure

(B) The distance around a 3D figure

(C) The total area of all faces of a 3D figure

(D) The height of a 3D figure

23. *Find the volume of a rectangular prism with dimensions 9 cm by 5 cm by 4 cm.*

Your Answer:

Find more at
ViewMath.com/KS-Grade7

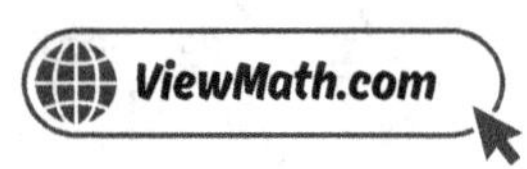

24. The diagram below shows four different sampling methods used to survey students at a school. Which method is most likely to produce an unbiased sample?

Method A
Survey the football team

Method B
Survey every 10th student on the school roster

Method C
Post survey online and wait for responses

Method D
Survey students in one math class

(A) Method A

(B) Method B

(C) Method C

(D) Method D

25. Class A: median 90, IQR 6. Class B: median 83, IQR 14. Which class is more consistent?

Your Answer

26. Class A: median 85, IQR 8, range 20. Class B: median 80, IQR 15, range 40. A student says "Class B is better because it has a wider range." Is the student correct?

(A) Yes — wider range means more talent

(B) No — wider range means less consistency, and Class A has a higher median

(C) Yes — Class B's scores spread more, which is always better

(D) No — range does not measure anything useful

Find more at
ViewMath.com/KS-Grade7

27. Look at the probability scale below. Point P is marked on the scale. A bag contains some red and blue marbles. If the probability of drawing a red marble is at point P, how many red marbles could be in a bag of 20 marbles?

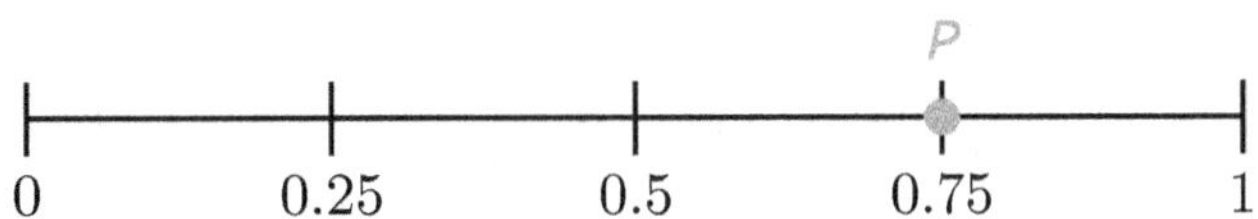

Your Answer:

28. Which of the following is an example of a uniform probability model?

(A) A bag with 3 red, 5 blue, and 2 green marbles

(B) A fair number cube with 6 sides

(C) A spinner with sections of different sizes

(D) A weighted coin

29. A coin is flipped and a die is rolled. What is the probability of getting heads and a number greater than 4?

(A) $\frac{1}{12}$

(B) $\frac{1}{6}$

(C) $\frac{2}{12}$

(D) $\frac{1}{3}$

30. A game has a 25% chance of winning. Which simulation model correctly represents this?

(A) Flip a coin — heads means win

(B) Roll a die — roll a 1 means win

(C) Use a spinner with 4 equal sections — one section means win

(D) Use digits 0–9 — digits 0–4 mean win

⭐ *End of Practice Test 7* ⭐

Great job finishing the test!

 *My Score*

I got _____________ out of 30 questions right.

*Check your answers in the **Answer Key** at the back of the book.*

 *Review any questions you missed. That's how we learn!*

📊 *Check Your Score Online!*

*Visit **ViewMath Academy** to enter your answers and see which topics you need to review. You can also explore lessons, take quizzes, track your scores, and save your progress!*

viewmath.com/score/7.1.KS.22

Or go to viewmath.com/score and enter code: 7.1.KS.22

Practice Test 8

📋 *30 Questions*

✏️ Before You Start ✏️

- ✔ **Read each question carefully** before choosing your answer.
- ✔ **Show your work** on scratch paper when you need to.
- ✔ **Skip hard questions** and come back to them later.
- ✔ **Check your answers** when you're done.
- ✔ **Take your time** — there's no rush!

⭐ **You've Got This!** ⭐

Do your best and show what you know!

1. A car travels at a constant speed. It goes 150 miles in 2.5 hours. What is the constant of proportionality?

(A) 30 mph

(B) 60 mph

(C) 75 mph

(D) 150 mph

2. Two friends start walking at the same time. The graph shows their distances. How many miles apart are they after 6 hours?

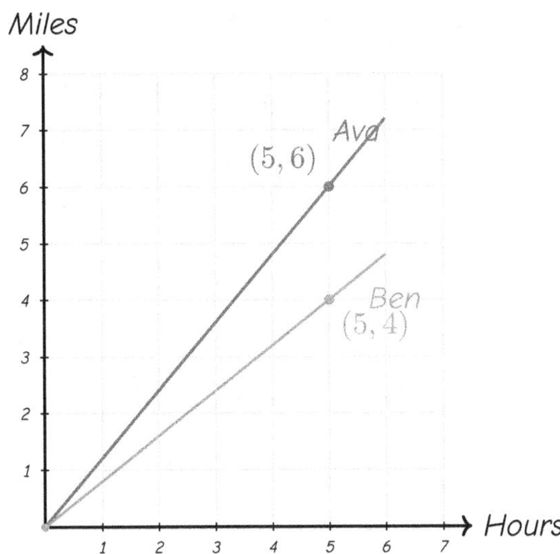

Your Answer:

3. A scale drawing uses 1 cm = 4.5 m. If a building is 27 m tall, how tall is it in the drawing?

Your Answer:

4. What is 150% of 40?

(A) 20

(B) 40

(C) 50

(D) 60

5. *Estimate a 20% tip on a $93 bill. Round the bill first, then calculate.*

Your Answer:

6. The number line below shows an estimated value and an actual value. What is the percent error?

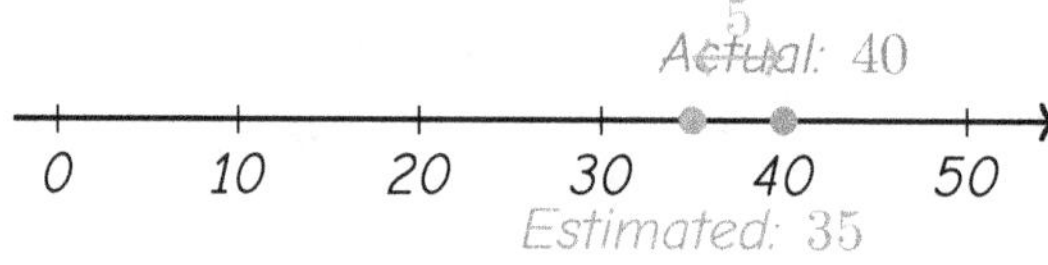

(A) 5%

(B) 10%

(C) 12.5%

(D) 14.3%

7. An elevator goes 3 floors up from the lobby, then 7 floors down. Which integer describes its final position relative to the lobby?

(A) 4

(B) −4

(C) 10

(D) −10

8. A bank account has −$50 (overdrawn). A deposit of $75 is made. What is the new balance?

(A) −$125

(B) −$25

(C) $25

(D) $125

9. Evaluate $-4y + 10$ when $y = 3$.

(A) 22

(B) −2

(C) 2

(D) −22

Find more at
ViewMath.com/KS-Grade7

ViewMath.com

10. Write an expression with three terms that simplifies to $4n + 7$.

Your Answer:

11. The table shows a pattern. What is the value of x when the output is 41?

Input (x)	Output
1	8
2	11
3	14
?	41

(A) $x = 12$

(B) $x = 11$

(C) $x = 13$

(D) $x = 14$

12. Solve $5(n + 3) = -10$.

(A) $n = -5$

(B) $n = 1$

(C) $n = -1$

(D) $n = -\dfrac{25}{5}$

13. Solve $\dfrac{5n}{6} + \dfrac{1}{3} = 3$.

Your Answer:

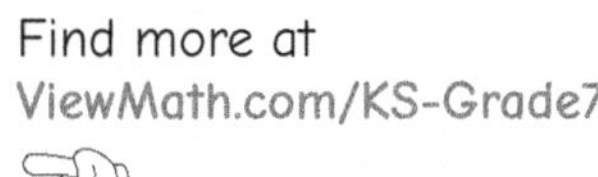

14. The table shows ticket prices for groups. A school has \$200 to spend and must also pay a \$35 bus fee. Write and solve an inequality to find the maximum number of students s who can go.

Group Size	Price per Student
1–10	\$12
11–25	\$9
26+	\$7

Assume the group qualifies for the \$9 rate.

Your Answer:

15. Solve $10 - 4x < 2$. Describe the graph.

Your Answer:

16. A map uses $1\ cm = 15\ km$. A trail is 8 cm on this map. On a new map, the trail is 24 cm. What is the scale ratio from old to new?

Your Answer:

17. How many different rectangles have an area of 24 cm^2 if the sides must be whole numbers?

Your Answer:

18. Two angles of a triangle are 60° and 60°, and the side between them is 5 cm. What type of triangle is formed?

(A) Right triangle

(B) Scalene triangle

(C) Equilateral triangle

(D) Obtuse triangle

Find more at
ViewMath.com/KS-Grade7

19. Name two different cross-section shapes you can get from slicing a cube.

Your Answer:

20. A square has a circle inscribed inside it as shown. The side of the square is 10 cm. What is the area of the circle? Use $\pi \approx 3.14$.

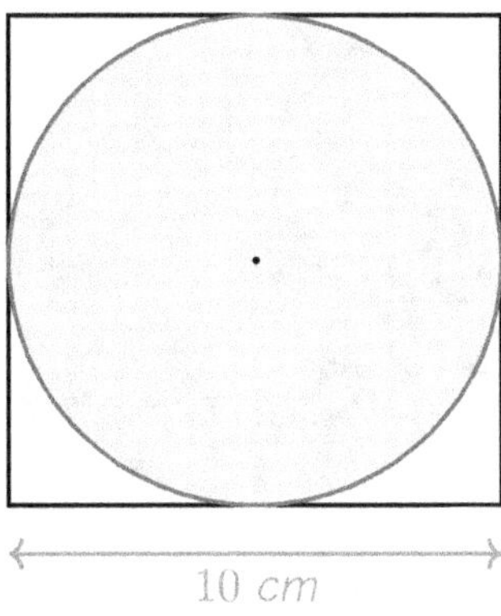

(A) 31.4 cm^2

(B) 78.5 cm^2

(C) 100 cm^2

(D) 314 cm^2

21. A rectangular patio is 12 ft by 8 ft. A circular hot tub with a diameter of 6 ft is placed on the patio. What is the area of the patio NOT covered by the hot tub? Use $\pi \approx 3.14$.

Your Answer:

22. What is the surface area of a rectangular prism with length 5 cm, width 3 cm, and height 2 cm?

(A) 30 cm^2

(B) 62 cm^2

(C) 46 cm^2

(D) 31 cm^2

23. What is the volume of a cube with side length 5 m?

(A) $15\ m^3$

(B) $25\ m^3$

(C) $125\ m^3$

(D) $150\ m^3$

24. A random sample of 50 apples from an orchard found that 6 were bruised. If the orchard has 3,000 apples, about how many are bruised?

Your Answer:

25. Team A: mean 60, MAD 4. Team B: mean 70, MAD 3. Is the difference in means meaningful? Explain briefly.

Your Answer:

26. Data set: $20, 22, 25, 27, 30, 32, 35$. What is the IQR?

(A) 15

(B) 10

(C) 7

(D) 5

27. A spinner has 5 equal sections: red, blue, green, yellow, and white. What is the probability of landing on blue or green? Write your answer as a decimal.

Your Answer:

Find more at
ViewMath.com/KS-Grade7

28. A bag contains 5 yellow and 5 purple marbles. Lisa picks a marble, records the color, and replaces it 40 times. She gets yellow 24 times. Which statement is correct?

(A) The model predicts $P(yellow) = 0.5$, and the experiment gives $P(yellow) = 0.6$, so there is a small difference

(B) The model is wrong because $24 \neq 20$

(C) The model predicts $P(yellow) = 0.6$

(D) The experiment proves yellow is more likely than purple

29. A coin is flipped and a die is rolled. What is the probability of getting tails and a 1? Write your answer as a fraction.

Your Answer

30. How does increasing the number of trials in a simulation affect the results?

(A) The results become less reliable

(B) The experimental probability gets closer to the theoretical probability

(C) The results stay exactly the same

(D) The simulation takes less time

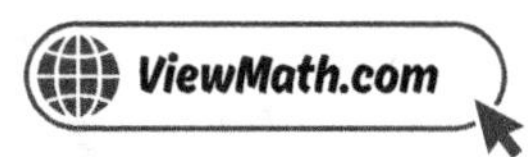

 # End of Practice Test 8 

Great job finishing the test!

 My Score

I got _____________ out of 30 questions right.

Check your answers in the **Answer Key** at the back of the book.

💡 Review any questions you missed. That's how we learn!

📊 Check Your Score Online!

Visit **ViewMath Academy** to enter your answers and see which topics you need to review. You can also explore lessons, take quizzes, track your scores, and save your progress!

viewmath.com/score/7.1.KS.23

Or go to viewmath.com/score and enter code: 7.1.KS.23

Practice Test 9

 *30 Questions*

 Before You Start 

- ✓ **Read each question carefully** before choosing your answer.
- ✓ **Show your work** on scratch paper when you need to.
- ✓ **Skip hard questions** and come back to them later.
- ✓ **Check your answers** when you're done.
- ✓ **Take your time** — there's no rush!

 **You've Got This!** 

Do your best and show what you know!

1. Two students find k from the point $(8, 20)$. Student A says $k = 2.5$. Student B says $k = 0.4$. Who is correct?

(A) Student A, because $k = \frac{y}{x}$

(B) Student B, because $k = \frac{x}{y}$

(C) Both are correct, depending on which variable is independent

(D) Neither is correct

2. The equation $y = 5x$ gives the cost of movie tickets. What does the point $(1, 5)$ represent?

(A) 5 movies cost \$1

(B) 1 ticket costs \$5

(C) The total for all tickets is \$5

(D) You need 5 hours to buy 1 ticket

3. A printer prints 120 pages in 8 minutes. How long will it take to print 450 pages?

(A) 25 min

(B) 28 min

(C) 30 min

(D) 36 min

4. 14 is what percent of 56?

(A) 14%

(B) 20%

(C) 25%

(D) 28%

5. A hair stylist charges \$55 for a haircut. The customer leaves a 20% tip. What is the total the customer pays?

(A) \$11.00

(B) \$60.50

(C) \$66.00

(D) \$75.00

6. *A builder estimated a project would cost $8,000. The actual cost was $7,500. What is the percent error?*

(A) 5%

(B) 6.25%

(C) 6.67%

(D) 10%

7. *Which expression equals 0?*

(A) $7 + 7$

(B) $7 - 7$

(C) $7 \times 0 + 7$

(D) $|-7| - |7|$

8. *A thermometer shows temperature changes over three hours.*

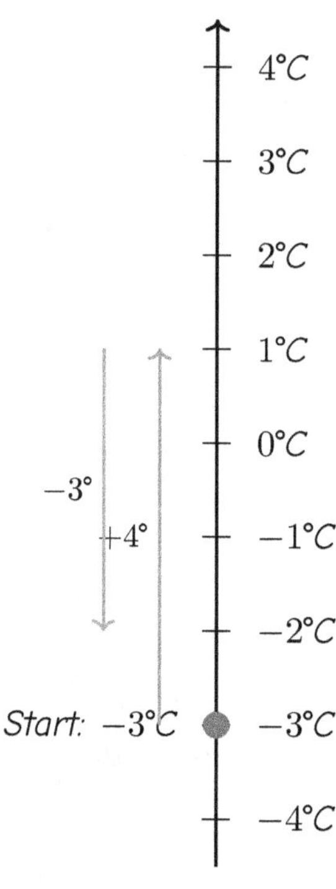

What is the final temperature after these two changes?

Your Answer:

9. *Which phrase best describes the expression* $5n - 8$*?*

(A) 8 less than 5 times a number   (B) 5 less than 8 times a number

(C) 8 minus 5 times a number   (D) 5 times a number less 8 times that number

10. *A rectangular garden has the dimensions shown. Write a simplified expression for the total distance around the garden (its perimeter).*

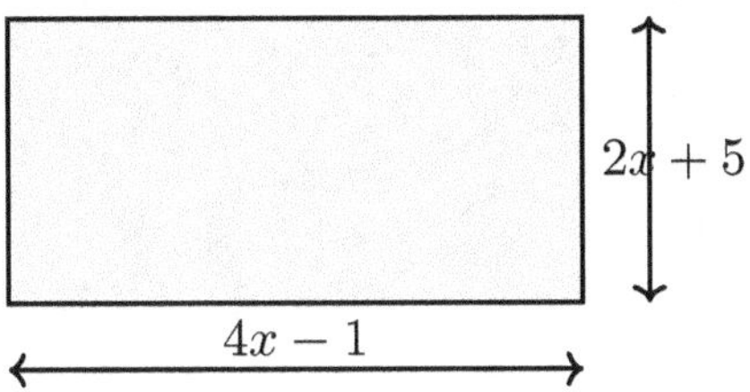

Your Answer:

11. *Which equation has the solution* $x = 5$*?*

(A) $4x + 3 = 18$ (B) $4x + 3 = 23$

(C) $4x - 3 = 23$ (D) $4x - 5 = 25$

12. *Solve* $2(x + 6) = 20.$

(A) $x = 4$ (B) $x = 7$

(C) $x = 10$ (D) $x = 14$

13. A shirt is on sale for $\frac{2}{3}$ of its original price. After using a \$5 coupon, you pay \$15. What equation finds the original price p?

(A) $\frac{2}{3}p + 5 = 15$

(B) $p - \frac{2}{3} - 5 = 15$

(C) $\frac{2}{3}p - 5 = 15$

(D) $\frac{2}{3}(p - 5) = 15$

14. Solve $-3n + 6 \leq 0$.

(A) $n \leq 2$

(B) $n \leq -2$

(C) $n \geq 2$

(D) $n \geq -2$

15. Solve $\frac{x}{2} - 3 > 1$ and describe the graph.

(A) Open circle at 8, shade right

(B) Closed circle at 8, shade right

(C) Open circle at 4, shade right

(D) Open circle at 8, shade left

16. A blueprint uses $1\ in = 12\ ft$. You redraw at $1\ in = 4\ ft$. A door that is $0.5\ in$ wide on the original becomes how wide?

(A) $0.5\ in$

(B) $1\ in$

(C) $1.5\ in$

(D) $3\ in$

17. A rectangle must have a perimeter of $24\ cm$. How many different rectangles can satisfy this condition?

(A) None

(B) Exactly one

(C) Exactly two

(D) More than one

18. Two sides of a triangle are 9 cm and 12 cm with an included angle of 60°. What type of condition is this?

(A) SSS

(B) SAS

(C) ASA

(D) AAA

19. You cut a cone with a vertical slice through its apex (tip). What shape is the cross-section?

(A) Circle

(B) Triangle

(C) Rectangle

(D) Semicircle

20. A quarter-circle has a radius of 8 cm. What is its area? Use $\pi \approx 3.14$.

(A) $200.96 \ cm^2$

(B) $100.48 \ cm^2$

(C) $50.24 \ cm^2$

(D) $25.12 \ cm^2$

21. A pentagon can be divided into a rectangle 6 cm by 4 cm and a triangle with base 6 cm and height 2 cm. What is the total area?

(A) $24 \ cm^2$

(B) $30 \ cm^2$

(C) $36 \ cm^2$

(D) $48 \ cm^2$

22. What is the surface area of a cube with side length 4 cm?

(A) $16 \ cm^2$

(B) $64 \ cm^2$

(C) $96 \ cm^2$

(D) $24 \ cm^2$

Find more at
ViewMath.com/KS-Grade7

23. A rectangular prism has a base area of 24 cm^2 and a height of 7 cm. What is its volume?

(A) 31 cm^3

(B) 168 cm^3

(C) 336 cm^3

(D) 17 cm^3

24. A researcher wants to know the average height of seventh graders in a state. She measures the heights of 100 seventh graders from different schools. What is the sample?

(A) All seventh graders in the state

(B) All students in the schools she visited

(C) The 100 seventh graders she measured

(D) The tallest seventh graders

25. The box plots below compare test scores for Class A and Class B.

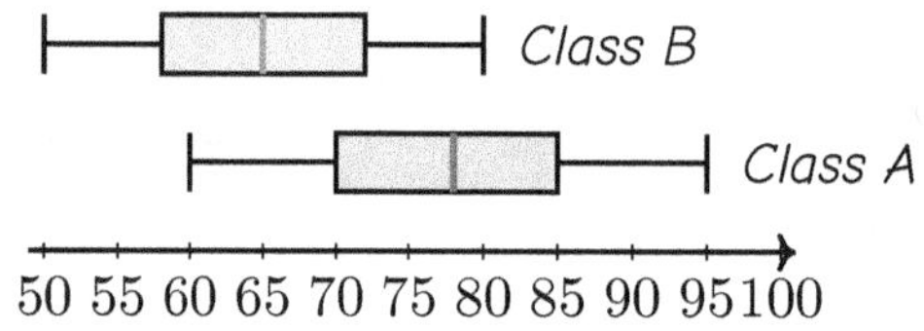

Which statement is best supported by the box plots?

(A) Class B scored higher than Class A

(B) Class A has a higher median and a larger IQR

(C) Class A has a higher median and both classes have the same IQR

(D) Class A and Class B overlap, but Class A's median is higher

26. Group A: $\{60, 65, 70, 75, 80\}$. Group B: $\{40, 55, 70, 85, 100\}$. Both have a mean of 70. Which group is more variable?

(A) Group A

(B) Group B

(C) They are equally variable

(D) Cannot be determined

Find more at
ViewMath.com/KS-Grade7

27. The bar graph below shows the contents of a bag of marbles. What is the probability of randomly drawing a blue marble?

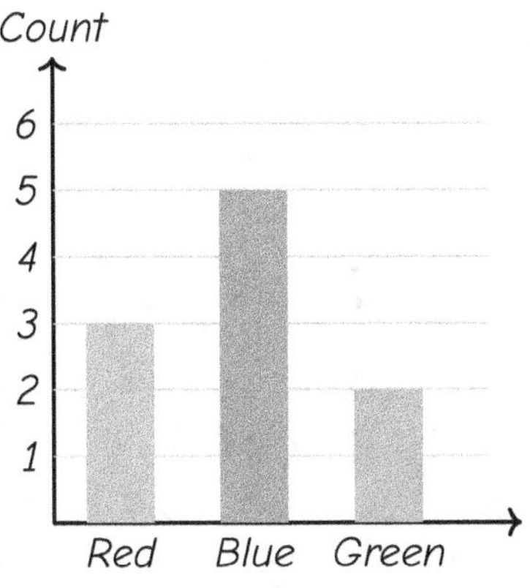

(A) $\frac{3}{10}$

(B) $\frac{1}{2}$

(C) $\frac{5}{10}$

(D) $\frac{2}{10}$

28. A teacher predicted that a spinner would land on red $\frac{1}{4}$ of the time. After 80 spins, red appeared 25 times. How do the observed and predicted results compare?

(A) They are very different — the model is wrong

(B) The observed ($\frac{25}{80} = 0.3125$) is close to the predicted (0.25)

(C) The observed result is exactly equal to the predicted result

(D) The predicted probability is higher than the observed

29. Three coins are flipped. What is the probability of getting NO heads (all tails)?

(A) $\frac{1}{2}$

(B) $\frac{1}{4}$

(C) $\frac{1}{8}$

(D) $\frac{3}{8}$

30. Describe how to use a standard die to simulate a $\frac{1}{3}$ probability event.

Your Answer:

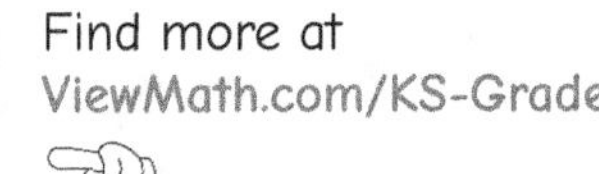

 # End of Practice Test 9 

Great job finishing the test!

 My Score

I got ___________ out of 30 questions right.

*Check your answers in the **Answer Key** at the back of the book.*

Review any questions you missed. That's how we learn!

Check Your Score Online!

Visit **ViewMath Academy** to enter your answers and see which topics you need to review. You can also explore lessons, take quizzes, track your scores, and save your progress!

viewmath.com/score/7.1.KS.24

Or go to viewmath.com/score and enter code: 7.1.KS.24

Practice Test 10

☑ 30 Questions

✏ Before You Start ✏

- ✓ **Read each question carefully** before choosing your answer.
- ✓ **Show your work** on scratch paper when you need to.
- ✓ **Skip hard questions** and come back to them later.
- ✓ **Check your answers** when you're done.
- ✓ **Take your time** — there's no rush!

⭐ You've Got This! ⭐

Do your best and show what you know!

1. The graph below shows a proportional relationship. What is the constant of proportionality?

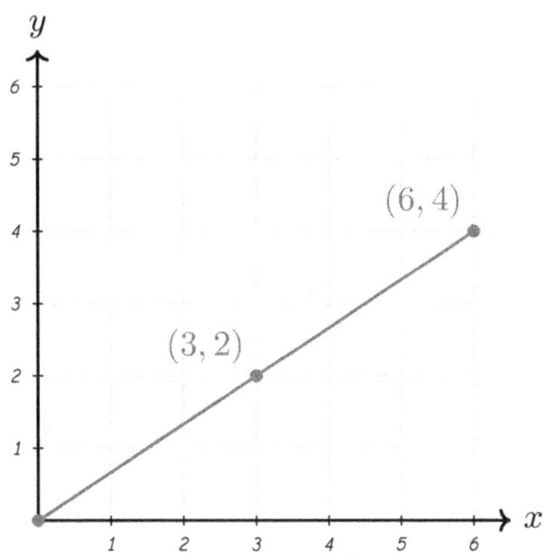

(A) $k = \frac{1}{2}$

(B) $k = \frac{2}{3}$

(C) $k = \frac{3}{2}$

(D) $k = 2$

2. The graph below shows a proportional relationship between hours and miles traveled. What is the unit rate?

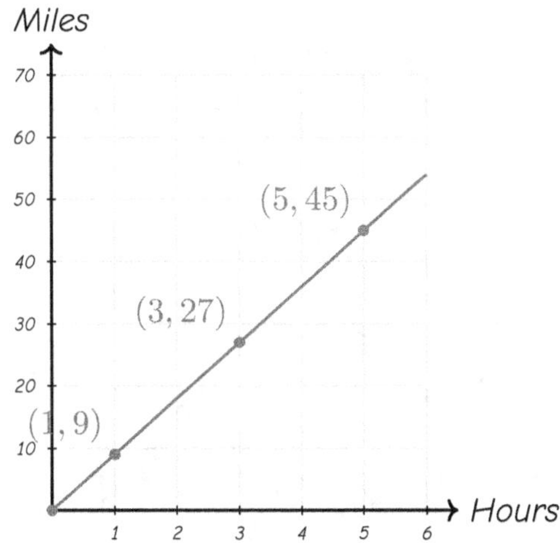

(A) 3 mph

(B) 9 mph

(C) 27 mph

(D) 45 mph

3. A map scale says 2 cm = 15 miles. Two cities are 7 cm apart on the map. What is the actual distance?

(A) 42.5 miles

(B) 45 miles

(C) 52.5 miles

(D) 105 miles

4. A library has 480 books. If 35% are fiction, how many fiction books does the library have?

(A) 148

(B) 160

(C) 168

(D) 172

5. Two friends split a $70 dinner bill equally and each leave a 15% tip on their share. How much does each person pay in total?

(A) $35.00

(B) $37.25

(C) $40.25

(D) $45.50

6. The bar graph shows the estimated and actual amounts of water (in liters) collected during an experiment over three days. On which day was the percent error the largest, and what was it?

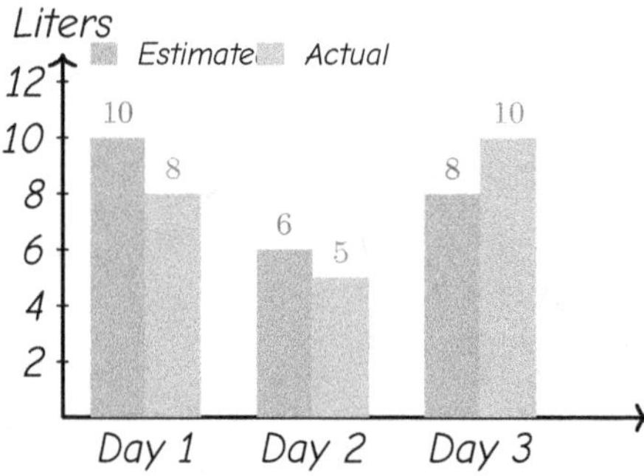

Your Answer:

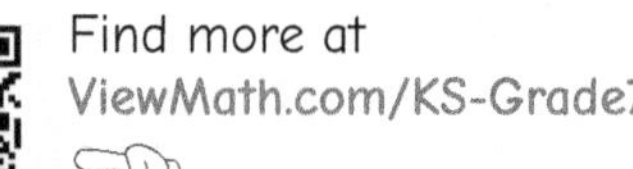

7. Find $|-23|$.

Your Answer:

8. What is $(-18) + 18$?

Your Answer:

9. Evaluate $2a + 7$ when $a = -3$.

A) 13

B) 1

C) -13

D) -1

10. Simplify $3y + 8 - 5y - 2$.

A) $8y + 6$

B) $-2y + 6$

C) $2y - 6$

D) $-2y + 10$

11. The bar model shows an equation. Solve for x.

45			
x	x	x	6

Your Answer:

12. *Solve* $2(4x - 3) = 26$.

  (A) $x = 3$ (B) $x = 4$

  (C) $x = 2$ (D) $x = 5$

13. *The bar graph shows how much three students earned. Together they earned a total of $31.50. Student C earned* $\dfrac{1}{2}$ *as much as Student A. Find how much Student C earned.*

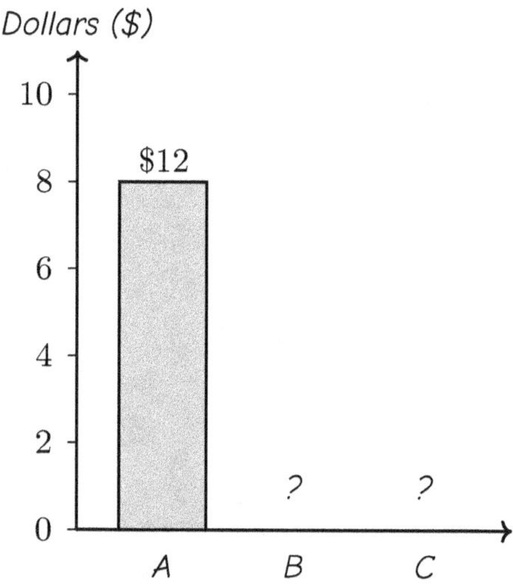

Student A earned $12, and Student C earned $\dfrac{1}{2}$ of Student A's earnings.

Your Answer

14. *Solve* $-x + 9 \leq 15$.

  (A) $x \leq -6$ (B) $x \geq 6$

  (C) $x \geq -6$ (D) $x \leq 6$

15. Solve $6 - 2x \leq -4$ and describe the graph.

(A) Closed circle at 5, shade right   (B) Open circle at 5, shade right

(C) Closed circle at 5, shade left   (D) Closed circle at -5, shade right

16. A drawing uses $1\ cm = 12\ m$. You redraw at $1\ cm = 4\ m$. A hallway is 5 cm on the original. How long is it on the new drawing?

Your Answer:

17. A circle with radius 5 cm is described as a condition. How many circles satisfy this condition?

(A) None   (B) Exactly one

(C) More than one (different positions)   (D) It depends on the center location

18. Look at the triangle below. Two sides and the included angle are given. What is the condition type, and is the triangle unique?

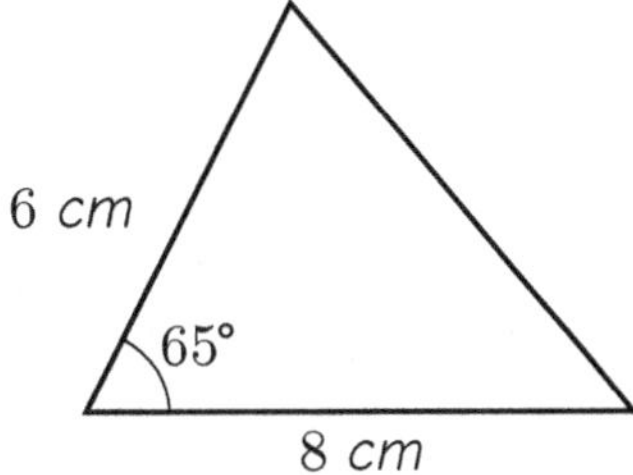

Your Answer:

19. A cube can be sliced to produce a hexagonal cross-section. How?

(A) By cutting parallel to the base   (B) By cutting diagonally through all six faces

(C) By cutting vertically through the center   (D) It is impossible to get a hexagon from a cube

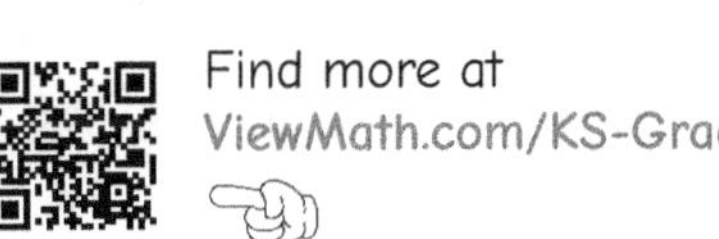
Find more at
ViewMath.com/KS-Grade7

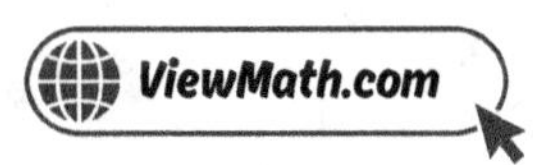

20. A pizza has a radius of 7 inches. What is the area of the pizza? Use $\pi \approx \frac{22}{7}$.

(A) $44\ in^2$

(B) $154\ in^2$

(C) $308\ in^2$

(D) $22\ in^2$

21. A composite shape is made of a rectangle that is 10 cm by 4 cm and a triangle with base 10 cm and height 3 cm attached to one side. What is the total area?

(A) $40\ cm^2$

(B) $55\ cm^2$

(C) $70\ cm^2$

(D) $120\ cm^2$

22. A cereal box is 30 cm tall, 20 cm wide, and 6 cm deep. What is its surface area?

(A) $1,440\ cm^2$

(B) $1,560\ cm^2$

(C) $1,800\ cm^2$

(D) $3,600\ cm^2$

23. A rectangular prism has a volume of $360\ cm^3$. Its length is 12 cm and its height is 5 cm. What is its width?

Your Answer

24. The table below shows the results of two samples taken from a population of 1,000 students.

	Sample 1 (50 students)	Sample 2 (50 students)
Prefer Math	18	22
Prefer Science	14	12
Prefer English	10	8
Prefer Art	8	8

Based on both samples, the best prediction for how many of the 1,000 students prefer math is:

(A) 180

(B) 220

(C) 400

(D) 360

25. Two histograms show that Group A's data is skewed left and Group B's data is symmetric. Which measure of center is most appropriate to compare them?

(A) Mean for both

(B) Median for both

(C) Mode for both

(D) Range for both

26. Data: $100, 200, 300, 400, 500$. Find the median and the IQR.

Your Answer:

27. What does a probability of 1 mean?

(A) The event is impossible

(B) The event is unlikely

(C) The event has a 50% chance

(D) The event is certain to happen

28. *Look at the spinner below. Which probability model correctly represents this spinner?*

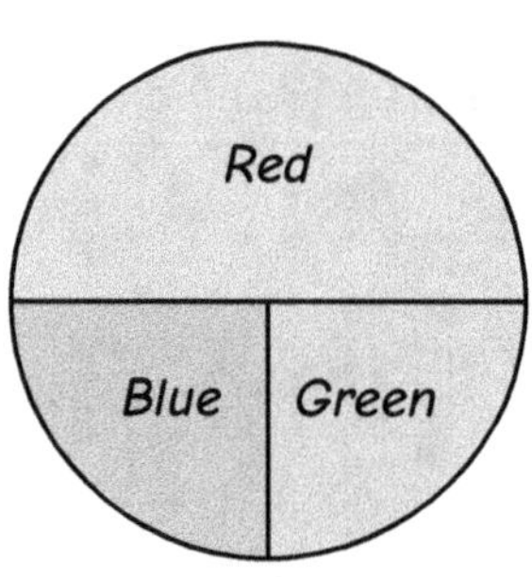

(A) $P(Red) = \frac{1}{3}$, $P(Blue) = \frac{1}{3}$, $P(Green) = \frac{1}{3}$

(B) $P(Red) = \frac{1}{2}$, $P(Blue) = \frac{1}{4}$, $P(Green) = \frac{1}{4}$

(C) $P(Red) = \frac{1}{4}$, $P(Blue) = \frac{1}{4}$, $P(Green) = \frac{1}{2}$

(D) $P(Red) = \frac{1}{2}$, $P(Blue) = \frac{1}{2}$, $P(Green) = 0$

29. *Two dice are rolled. What is the probability that the product (not the sum) of the two numbers is 12?*

(A) $\frac{2}{36}$

(B) $\frac{4}{36}$

(C) $\frac{3}{36}$

(D) $\frac{6}{36}$

30. *A student simulates rolling two dice 36 times to see how often the sum is 7. They get a sum of 7 a total of 8 times. How does this compare to the expected number?*

(A) *Expected: 6; the simulation result (8) is slightly higher*

(B) *Expected: 6; the simulation result (8) is much higher*

(C) *Expected: 12; the simulation result (8) is lower*

(D) *Expected: 7; the simulation result (8) is exact*

 End of Practice Test 10 

Great job finishing the test!

 My Score

I got _____________ out of 30 questions right.

Check your answers in the **Answer Key** at the back of the book.

💡 Review any questions you missed. That's how we learn!

📊 Check Your Score Online!

Visit **ViewMath Academy** to enter your answers and see which topics you need to review. You can also explore lessons, take quizzes, track your scores, and save your progress!

viewmath.com/score/7.1.KS.25

Or go to viewmath.com/score and enter code: 7.1.KS.25

Answer Key & Explanations

Answer Key

First try each test on your own, then check your work here.

✔ Practice Test 1 — Answer Key

 $k = 2.5$; missing $x = 6$  B    A    C    B    $\approx 4.2\%$  B    C

9 6   10 $\frac{5}{4}x - 2$ or $1\frac{1}{4}x - 2$ 11 A   12 $t = \$14$ 13 $p = \$60$ 14 A   15 $x \geq -6$

16 A   17 Equilateral triangle   18 AAA   19 B   20 B   21 B   22 A   23 C

24 B   25 C   26 B   27 A   28 0.4   29 B   30 48

💡 Time to Learn! 💡

*Review the explanations below, **especially for the questions you missed.***

Understanding why each answer is correct builds stronger problem-solving skills.

***Tip:** Circle any questions you got wrong, then read their explanation carefully.*

📖 Practice Test 1 — Detailed Explanations

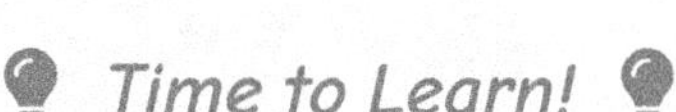 $k = \frac{7.5}{3} = 2.5$. For the missing row: $15 = 2.5x$ so $x = 15 \div 2.5 = 6$.

Find more at
ViewMath.com/KS-Grade7

 ViewMath.com

2   Line P: $k = \frac{7}{5} = 1.4$. Line Q: $k = \frac{6}{6} = 1$. Line P is steeper and has the greater unit rate.

3   Worker A: $60 \div 5 = 12$ boxes/hr. Worker B: $45 \div 5 = 9$ boxes/hr. Worker A is faster by $12 - 9 = 3$ boxes/hr.

4 $60\% = 0.60$. Multiply: $0.60 \times 300 = 180$ items.

5   Commission: $6{,}000 \times 0.05 = \$300$. Total: $400 + 300 = \$700$.

6 $\frac{|5-4.8|}{4.8} \times 100 = \frac{0.2}{4.8} \times 100 \approx 4.17 \approx 4.2\%$.

7   Point P is at -4 and Q is at 4. They are the same distance from 0 on opposite sides, so they are opposites.

8   Adding 0 to any number gives that number. $0 + (-7) = -7$.

9   Substitute: $\frac{5^2-1}{4} = \frac{25-1}{4} = \frac{24}{4} = 6$.

10   Find a common denominator: $\frac{2}{4}x + \frac{3}{4}x = \frac{5}{4}x$. The constant stays: $\frac{5}{4}x - 2$.

11   Perimeter: $(2x+1) + (x+3) + (x+5) = 39$. Combine: $4x + 9 = 39$. Subtract 9: $4x = 30$. Divide by 4: $x = 7.5$.

12 $4(t + 3) = 68$. Divide by 4: $t + 3 = 17$. Subtract 3: $t = 14$. Each ticket costs $\$14$.

13   After $\frac{1}{4}$ markdown: $p - \frac{p}{4} = \frac{3p}{4}$. After subtracting \$8: $\frac{3p}{4} - 8 = 37$. Add 8: $\frac{3p}{4} = 45$. Multiply by $\frac{4}{3}$: $p = 60$.

14   Subtract 3: $2x > 8$. Divide by 2: $x > 4$.

15   Closed circle means -6 is included, shading right means values greater than or equal to -6: $x \geq -6$.

Find more at
ViewMath.com/KS-Grade7

16 Scale ratio: $\frac{3}{9} = \frac{1}{3}$. New length: $12 \times \frac{1}{3} = 4$ cm.

17 Two equal sides with a 60° included angle gives a triangle where all angles are 60° (isosceles with 60° forces equilateral). All three sides are 5 cm.

18 Three angles determine the shape but not the size. Infinitely many similar triangles can share the same three angle measures.

19 A plane that intersects exactly three faces of a rectangular prism creates a triangular cross-section (one edge on each of the three faces).

20 $r = 7$ cm. $A = \frac{22}{7} \times 49 = 154$ cm^2.

21 Rectangle: $12 \times 5 = 60$ cm^2. Triangle: $\frac{1}{2} \times 4 \times 5 = 10$ cm^2. Remaining: $60 - 10 = 50$ cm^2.

22 Two triangles: $2 \times \frac{1}{2} \times 6 \times 4 = 24$ cm^2. Three rectangles: $6 \times 10 + 5 \times 10 + 5 \times 10 = 60 + 50 + 50 = 160$ cm^2. Total: $24 + 160 = 184$ cm^2.

23 $V = 50 \times 30 \times 40 = 60{,}000$ cm^3.

24 $\frac{15}{60} = \frac{1}{4} = 25\%$. So 25% of 600 = 150.

25 A box plot shows the quartiles (Q_1 and Q_3), so you can read the IQR directly as $Q_3 - Q_1$.

26 Company X has smaller IQR (1.5 vs. 4) and range (4 vs. 8), meaning delivery times are more predictable.

27 There are 5 green out of 10. $P(\text{not green}) = 1 - \frac{5}{10} = 0.5$.

28 $P(Z) = 1 - 0.15 - 0.45 = 0.40$.

Find more at
ViewMath.com/KS-Grade7

29. $P(\text{spinner} = 3) = \frac{1}{4}$, $P(\text{die} = 3) = \frac{1}{6}$. $P = \frac{1}{4} \times \frac{1}{6} = \frac{1}{24}$.

30. $80 \times 0.60 = 48$.

✅ Practice Test 2 — Answer Key

1. B
2. 0.75 birdhouses per hour; 7.5 birdhouses in 10 hours
3. $37\frac{1}{2}$ cups
4. B
5. D
6. C
7. D
8. -5
9. C
10. $5a + 2b$
11. B
12. $x = -10$
13. $x = 14$
14. $x \le 10$
15. D
16. C
17. D
18. B
19. 6 cm by 4 cm
20. B
21. B
22. 156 cm^2
23. C
24. 4%
25. B
26. City A: mean = 66.6°F, range = 10°F. City B: mean = 68.2°F, range = 18°F. City A is more consistent.
27. C
28. B
29. C
30. B

💡 Time to Learn! 💡

*Review the explanations below, **especially for the questions you missed**.*

Understanding why each answer is correct builds stronger problem-solving skills.

***Tip:** Circle any questions you got wrong, then read their explanation carefully.*

📖 Practice Test 2 — Detailed Explanations

1. $k = \frac{54}{2} = 27$, $\frac{135}{5} = 27$, $\frac{216}{8} = 27$. The car gets 27 miles per gallon.

Find more at
ViewMath.com/KS-Grade7

2. $k = \frac{3}{4} = 0.75$. In 10 hours: $0.75 \times 10 = 7.5$ birdhouses.

3. $k = \frac{7.5}{3} = 2.5$ cups per batch. For 15 batches: $2.5 \times 15 = 37.5 = 37\frac{1}{2}$ cups.

4. $75\% = 0.75$. Multiply: $0.75 \times 32 = 24$ students passed.

5. $17.20 \div 86 = 0.20 = 20\%$.

6. A: $\frac{|180-200|}{200} = 10\%$. B: $\frac{|220-200|}{200} = 10\%$. Both have 10% error.

7. Absolute value is the distance from 0. Since -9 is 9 units from 0, $|-9| = 9$.

8. Group positives: $5 + 3 = 8$. Group negatives: $(-11) + (-2) = -13$. Combine: $8 + (-13) = -5$.

9. Substitute: $\frac{10}{2} - 4 = 5 - 4 = 1$.

10. Combine a-terms: $-2a + 7a = 5a$. Combine b-terms: $5b - 3b = 2b$. Result: $5a + 2b$.

11. Subtract 2: $6 = \frac{x}{3}$. Multiply by 3: $x = 18$. Check: $\frac{18}{3} + 2 = 6 + 2 = 8$ ✓.

12. Divide by 2: $x + 7 = -3$. Subtract 7: $x = -10$. Check: $2(-10 + 7) = 2(-3) = -6$ ✓.

13. Subtract 1.5: $\frac{x}{4} = 3.5$. Multiply by 4: $x = 14$. The point is at 14 on the number line.

14. Subtract 7: $\frac{x}{2} \leq 5$. Multiply by 2: $x \leq 10$.

15. Closed circle means the endpoint is included, shading left means less than or equal to: $x \leq 7$.

Find more at
ViewMath.com/KS-Grade7

16. Scale ratio: $\frac{20}{10} = 2$. Every length on the new drawing is 2 times the old one. The drawing gets bigger because each cm now represents fewer real km.

17. Three angles (AAA) determine the shape but not the size. You can draw infinitely many similar triangles of different sizes with these angles.

18. $7 + 10 = 17 > 15$ ✓, $7 + 15 = 22 > 10$ ✓, $10 + 15 = 25 > 7$ ✓. SSS with valid lengths gives one unique triangle.

19. A cut parallel to the base of a rectangular prism produces a rectangle identical to the base: 6 cm by 4 cm.

20. $r^2 = A \div \pi = 78.5 \div 3.14 = 25$. So $r = 5$ cm.

21. Rectangle: $25 \times 10 = 250$ m^2. Semicircle: $\frac{1}{2} \times 3.14 \times 5^2 = \frac{1}{2} \times 78.5 = 39.25$ m^2. Total: $250 + 39.25 = 289.25$ m^2.

22. Two triangles: $2 \times \frac{1}{2} \times 3 \times 4 = 12$ cm^2. Three rectangles: $3 \times 12 + 4 \times 12 + 5 \times 12 = 36 + 48 + 60 = 144$ cm^2. Total: $12 + 144 = 156$ cm^2.

23. $B = \frac{1}{2} \times 8 \times 3 = 12$ cm^2. $V = Bh = 12 \times 10 = 120$ cm^3.

24. $\frac{8}{200} = 0.04 = 4\%$.

25. Class 1 center ≈ 10. Class 2 center ≈ 13. Difference ≈ 3 push-ups. Class 2 is higher.

26. City A: $(62 + 64 + 64 + 66 + 66 + 66 + 68 + 68 + 70 + 72) \div 10 = 666 \div 10 = 66.6$. Range $= 72 - 62 = 10$. City B: $(58 + 60 + 64 + 66 + 68 + 70 + 72 + 74 + 74 + 76) \div 10 = 682 \div 10 = 68.2$. Range $= 76 - 58 = 18$. City A has the smaller range.

27. A probability of 0 means the event cannot happen — it is impossible.

Find more at
ViewMath.com/KS-Grade7

28 Each color should appear about 50 times (200×0.25). The results $(55, 48, 52, 45)$ are all close to 50, supporting the model.

29 Outcomes with at least one tail: HT, TH, TT — that is 3 out of 4. $P = \frac{3}{4}$.

30 With 4 equal sections, each should appear about 25 times in 100 spins. The results $(26, 24, 28, 22)$ are all close to 25, suggesting the spinner is fair.

✅ Practice Test 3 — Answer Key

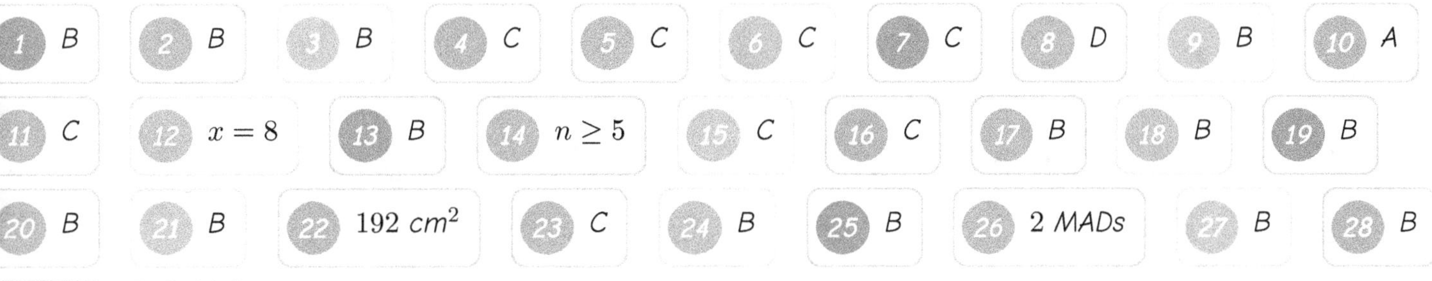

1 B	2 B	3 B	4 C	5 C	6 C	7 C	8 D	9 B	10 A
11 C	12 $x = 8$	13 B	14 $n \geq 5$	15 C	16 C	17 B	18 B	19 B	
20 B	21 B	22 $192\ cm^2$	23 C	24 B	25 B	26 2 MADs	27 B	28 B	
29 C	30 A								

💡 Time to Learn! 💡

Review the explanations below, **especially for the questions you missed**.

Understanding why each answer is correct builds stronger problem-solving skills.

Tip: Circle any questions you got wrong, then read their explanation carefully.

📖 Practice Test 3 — Detailed Explanations

1 If $k = \frac{3}{4}$, then $y = \frac{3}{4}x$. For $x = 8$: $y = \frac{3}{4} \times 8 = 6$. So $(8, 6)$ works.

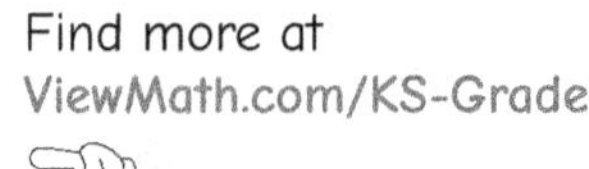
Find more at
ViewMath.com/KS-Grade7

2. *A steeper line means a higher slope, which equals a greater unit rate (constant of proportionality).*

3. *Store A:* $7.50 \div 3 = \$2.50$ *each. Store B:* $11.25 \div 5 = \$2.25$ *each. Store B is cheaper.*

4. *Divide:* $63 \div 0.90 = 70.$

5. *10% of \$78 = \$7.80. Half of that (5%) = \$3.90. Add:* $7.80 + 3.90 = \$11.70.$

6. $\frac{|4.5 - 5|}{5} \times 100 = \frac{0.5}{5} \times 100 = 10\%.$

7. *Both* $|10| = 10$ *and* $|-10| = 10.$ *Two numbers have the same absolute value: the number and its opposite.*

8. *A number plus its opposite (additive inverse) always equals 0.*

9. *Substitute:* $(-2)^2 + 3(-2) = 4 + (-6) = -2.$

10. $-6y + 4y = -2y.$ *Then* $-2y - y = -3y.$

11. *Subtract 9:* $3x = 21.$ *Divide by 3:* $x = 7.$ *Check:* $9 + 3(7) = 9 + 21 = 30$ ✓.

12. *Divide by 9:* $x - 3 = 5.$ *Add 3:* $x = 8.$ *Check:* $9(8 - 3) = 9(5) = 45$ ✓.

13. *Subtract 2:* $-0.4y = 4.$ *Divide by* -0.4: $y = -10.$ *Check:* $-0.4(-10) + 2 = 4 + 2 = 6$ ✓.

14. *Subtract 10:* $-5n \leq -25.$ *Divide by* -5 *and flip:* $n \geq 5.$

15. *Subtract 12:* $-3x \geq -12.$ *Divide by* -3 *and flip:* $x \leq 4.$ *Closed circle at 4, shade left.*

Find more at
ViewMath.com/KS-Grade7

16 Scale ratio: $\frac{60}{20} = 3$. Area scales by $3^2 = 9$. New area: $4 \times 9 = 36\ cm^2$.

17 Three side lengths that satisfy the triangle inequality (SSS) produce exactly one unique triangle. Check: $5 + 6 = 11 > 7$, $5 + 7 = 12 > 6$, $6 + 7 = 13 > 5$. All pass.

18 $90 + 45 + 45 = 180°$ ✓. But AAA alone allows different sizes. Many 45-45-90 triangles exist.

19 A vertical cut perpendicular to the triangular bases of a triangular prism produces a rectangle (the cut goes through the lateral faces).

20 $r = 8 \div 2 = 4\ ft$. $A = \pi r^2 = 3.14 \times 16 = 50.24\ ft^2$.

21 Triangle: $\frac{1}{2} \times 6 \times 8 = 24\ cm^2$. Rectangle: $8 \times 3 = 24\ cm^2$. Total: $24 + 24 = 48\ cm^2$.

22 The prism is $10 \times 4 \times 4$. $SA = 2(10 \times 4) + 2(10 \times 4) + 2(4 \times 4) = 80 + 80 + 32 = 192\ cm^2$.

23 $B = \frac{1}{2}(4 + 6) \times 3 = 15\ cm^2$. $V = 15 \times 10 = 150\ cm^3$.

24 Larger random samples better represent the population and give more reliable results.

25 Difference in medians: $88 - 82 = 6$. In MADs: $\frac{6}{4} = 1.5$ MADs.

26 Difference: $57 - 45 = 12$. In MADs: $\frac{12}{6} = 2$.

27 The letters in MATH are M, A, T, H. Only A is a vowel. $P = \frac{1}{4}$.

28 The probability of drawing red $(\frac{4}{5})$ is different from drawing blue $(\frac{1}{5})$, so this is a non-uniform model.

29　The only way to get a sum of 2 is $(1, 1)$. $P = \frac{1}{36}$.

30　$P = \frac{6}{40} = 0.15$. The theoretical probability is $\frac{1}{8} = 0.125$, close to the simulation result.

✅ Practice Test 4 — Answer Key

1　B　　2　$112.50　　3　B　　4　110　　5　C　　6　C　　7　C　　8　15 feet　　9　C

10　A　　11　A　　12　$x = 5$　　13　A　　14　$x \leq -5$　　15　C　　16　C　　17　B　　18　C

19　C　　20　D　　21　B　　22　C　　23　B　　24　Random variation (or the sample may be biased)

25　C　　26　B　　27　C　　28　C　　29　$\frac{3}{8}$　　30　B

💡 Time to Learn! 💡

Review the explanations below, **especially for the questions you missed.**

Understanding why each answer is correct builds stronger problem-solving skills.

Tip: Circle any questions you got wrong, then read their explanation carefully.

📖 Practice Test 4 — Detailed Explanations

1　$k = \frac{y}{x} = \frac{12}{3} = 4$. Check: $\frac{20}{5} = 4$ and $\frac{32}{8} = 4$.

2　$k = \frac{67.50}{3} = 22.50$ per hour. Cost for 5 hours: $22.50 \times 5 = \$112.50$.

3 Factory 1: $168 \div 7 = 24$ items/hr. Factory 2: $200 \div 8 = 25$ items/hr. Factory 2 is more productive.

4 $44\% = 0.44$. Multiply: $0.44 \times 250 = 110$ chocolate candies.

5 $15\% = 0.15$. Tip: $40 \times 0.15 = \$6.00$.

6 Absolute value ensures the percent error is positive whether the estimate was too high or too low.

7 Absolute value measures distance from 0, which is always ≥ 0. It can never be negative.

8 $(-30) + 45 = 15$. She is now 15 feet above sea level.

9 "The product of 7 and p" is $7p$. "Decreased by 12" means subtract 12: $7p - 12$.

10 $7x$ and $3x$ are like terms. Add the coefficients: $7 + 3 = 10$. Result: $10x$.

11 Subtract 12: $\frac{w}{5} = 8$. Multiply by 5: $w = 40$. Check: $\frac{40}{5} + 12 = 8 + 12 = 20$ ✓.

12 Divide by 5: $2x - 3 = 7$. Add 3: $2x = 10$. Divide by 2: $x = 5$. Check: $5(2(5) - 3) = 5(7) = 35$ ✓.

13 If $\frac{2}{3}x = 8$, then each $\frac{1}{3}$ of x is 4. So $x = 3 \times 4 = 12$.

14 Subtract 8: $-3x \geq 15$. Divide by -3 and flip: $x \leq -5$.

15 Divide by -2 and flip: $x \geq -5$. Closed circle at -5, shade right.

16 Scale ratio: $\frac{4}{2} = 2$. New base: $5 \times 2 = 10$ cm.

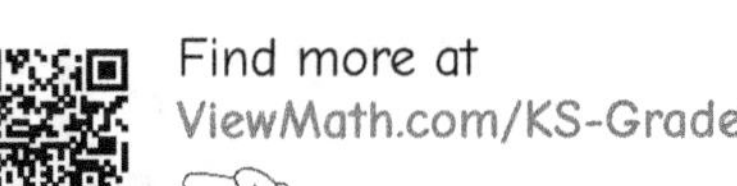
Find more at
ViewMath.com/KS-Grade7

17 AAA with a specified side length fixes the size. A 60°-60°-60° triangle is equilateral, so all sides are 4 cm. Exactly one triangle.

18 Although $90 + 100 + (-10) = 180$, every angle in a triangle must be greater than 0°. A negative angle is impossible.

19 A rectangular prism has flat faces and straight edges. Its cross-sections can be triangles, rectangles, pentagons, or hexagons, but never circles (since it has no curved surfaces).

20 $A = \pi r^2 = 3.14 \times 100 = 314 \ cm^2$.

21 Square: $8^2 = 64 \ cm^2$. Semicircle: $\frac{1}{2} \times \pi r^2 = \frac{1}{2} \times 3.14 \times 16 = 25.12 \ cm^2$. Total: $64 + 25.12 = 89.12 \ cm^2$.

22 The three pairs of faces have areas $7 \times 4 = 28$, $7 \times 3 = 21$, and $4 \times 3 = 12 \ m^2$. The largest is $28 \ m^2$.

23 Bottom row: 5 cubes. Second row: 3 cubes. Third row: 3 cubes. Total: $5 + 3 + 3 = 11 \ cm^3$.

24 Even a well-chosen random sample may differ slightly from the population due to chance.

25 A complete comparison requires looking at both center (where the data clusters) and spread (how spread out it is).

26 Difference $= \$620 - \$500 = \$120$. In MADs: $\frac{120}{40} = 3$ MADs.

27 $\frac{3}{4} = 0.75$, which is close to 1. The team is likely to win, but since the probability is not 1, it is not certain.

28 $P(tails) = 1 - 0.60 = 0.40$. Since heads and tails have different probabilities, this is a non-uniform model.

29 Outcomes with exactly 2 tails: HTT, THT, TTH — that is 3 out of 8. $P = \frac{3}{8}$.

Find more at
ViewMath.com/KS-Grade7

30 Each coin flip has a 50% chance of heads (pass). Flipping 3 coins and counting exactly 2 heads simulates exactly 2 passes.

✅ Practice Test 5 — Answer Key

1 $k = 70$ widgets per hour	**2** B	**3** B

1 $k = 70$ widgets per hour **2** B **3** B **4** D **5** C **6** $\approx 7.1\%$ **7** C

8 C **9** B **10** $10x + 5$ **11** $x = 8$ **12** B **13** $x = 8$ **14** A **15** B

16 $96\ \text{cm}^2$ **17** D **18** C **19** C **20** C **21** $52\ \text{cm}^2$ **22** C **23** B **24** B

25 A **26** B **27** $\frac{5}{8}$ **28** C **29** $\frac{1}{9}$ **30** C

💡 Time to Learn! 💡

Review the explanations below, **especially for the questions you missed**.

Understanding why each answer is correct builds stronger problem-solving skills.

Tip: Circle any questions you got wrong, then read their explanation carefully.

📖 Practice Test 5 — Detailed Explanations

1 $k = \frac{175}{2.5} = 70$ widgets per hour.

2 Unit rate $= k = \frac{18}{3} = 6$.

3 12-oz: $3.60 \div 12 = \$0.30/\text{oz}$. 20-oz: $5.40 \div 20 = \$0.27/\text{oz}$. The 20-oz box is the better value.

Find more at
ViewMath.com/KS-Grade7

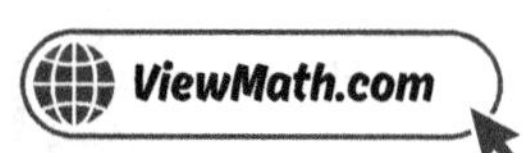

4 — The shaded portion is $3 \times 15 = 45$. The total is 75. Percent: $45 \div 75 = 0.60 = 60\%$.

5 — $250{,}000 \times 0.03 = \$7{,}500$.

6 — $\frac{|45-42|}{42} \times 100 = \frac{3}{42} \times 100 \approx 7.14 \approx 7.1\%$.

7 — On a number line, -7 is to the left of -4, so $-7 < -4$.

8 — $(-9) + n = -2$ means $n = -2 - (-9) = -2 + 9 = 7$.

9 — "The sum of k and 10" is $k + 10$. "Half" of that sum is $\frac{k+10}{2}$.

10 — Combine variable terms: $3x + 5x + 2x = 10x$. Combine constants: $2 - 1 + 4 = 5$. Perimeter: $10x + 5$.

11 — Subtract 15: $2x = 16$. Divide by 2: $x = 8$. Check: $2(8) + 15 = 31$ ✓.

12 — Divide by -4: $y + 3 = -7$. Subtract 3: $y = -10$. Check: $-4(-10 + 3) = -4(-7) = 28$ ✓.

13 — Subtract 4.2: $-0.3x = -2.4$. Divide by -0.3: $x = 8$. Check: $-0.3(8) + 4.2 = -2.4 + 4.2 = 1.8$ ✓.

14 — Current height plus growth: $42 + g > 48$.

15 — Open circle means -1 is not included, shading left means less than: $x < -1$.

16 — Scale ratio: $\frac{80}{20} = 4$. New dimensions: $2 \times 4 = 8$ cm and $3 \times 4 = 12$ cm. New area: $8 \times 12 = 96$ cm^2.

17 — Two side lengths of a parallelogram do not fix the angles. The shape can be a rectangle, a rhomboid, or anything in between. Many different parallelograms are possible.

Find more at
ViewMath.com/KS-Grade7

ViewMath.com

18. The three angles sum to 190°, not 180°. Triangle angles must always sum to exactly 180°.

19. A cone has a circular base, and all horizontal cuts parallel to the base produce circles of varying sizes.

20. $A = \pi r^2 = 3.14 \times 25 = 78.5\ m^2$.

21. Top: $10 \times 2 = 20\ cm^2$. Bottom: $10 \times 2 = 20\ cm^2$. Middle: $2 \times 6 = 12\ cm^2$. Total: $20 + 20 + 12 = 52\ cm^2$.

22. A rectangular prism has 6 faces: top, bottom, front, back, left, and right.

23. Space volume: $6 \times 4 \times 3 = 72\ ft^3$. Box volume: $2 \times 2 \times 3 = 12\ ft^3$. Number: $72 \div 12 = 6$ boxes.

24. The population is the entire group you want to study — all 800 students.

25. A smaller MAD means scores are closer to the mean, so Team A is more consistent.

26. Same mean means same center. Different MADs mean one group's data is more spread out than the other's.

27. $P(\text{not happening}) = 1 - \frac{3}{8} = \frac{5}{8}$.

28. There are 2 B tiles out of 5 total. $P(B) = \frac{2}{5}$.

29. Products of 6: $(1,6), (2,3), (3,2), (6,1)$ — 4 outcomes. $P = \frac{4}{36} = \frac{1}{9}$.

30. Before choosing a model or running trials, you must first identify what event you're simulating and what the possible outcomes are.

Find more at
ViewMath.com/KS-Grade7

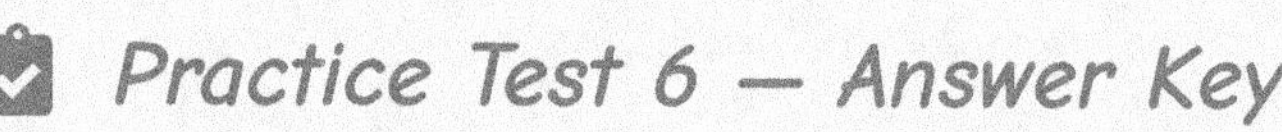 **Practice Test 6 — Answer Key**

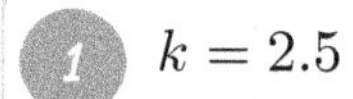 $k = 2.5$  C    C    D    C    C    C    A    C

 A   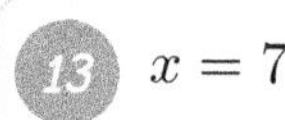 C    A $x = 7$ C   B   C

 Greater than 4 cm and less than 20 cm    Yes, unique; it is a right triangle    A    4 m

 A    1330 cm² ... D   C   B   B   C   B   C

 B

 💡 **Time to Learn!** 💡

Review the explanations below, **especially for the questions you missed**.

Understanding why each answer is correct builds stronger problem-solving skills.

Tip: Circle any questions you got wrong, then read their explanation carefully.

 📖 **Practice Test 6 — Detailed Explanations**

1. $k = \frac{y}{x} = \frac{15}{6} = 2.5$.

2. $k = \frac{10}{4} = 2.5$. When $x = 7$: $y = 2.5 \times 7 = 17.5$.

3. $\frac{3}{87} = \frac{x}{435}$. Cross-multiply: $87x = 1{,}305$, so $x = 15$ gallons.

4. Divide the part by the percent: $45 \div 0.75 = 60$.

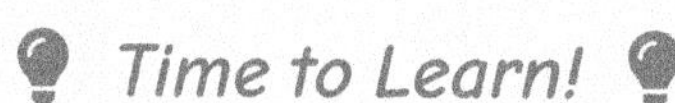

5. *Planning fee:* $4{,}000 \times 0.10 = \$400.$ *Coordination fee:* $4{,}000 \times 0.03 = \$120.$ *Total:* $400 + 120 = \$520.$

6. $\frac{|30-28|}{28} \times 100 = \frac{2}{28} \times 100 \approx 7.1\%.$

7. *The opposite of* 4 *is* $-4.$ *The opposite of* -4 *is* $4.$ *Taking the opposite twice returns you to the original number.*

8. $4 + (-10) = -6.$ *Check the others:* $(-3) + (-9) = -12;\ 8 + (-2) = 6;\ (-1) + (-4) = -5.$

9. *"Divided by 4" gives* $\frac{n}{4}.$ *"Increased by 3" means add 3:* $\frac{n}{4} + 3.$

10. *Combine variable terms:* $-4x + 7x = 3x.$ *Combine constants:* $9 - 3 = 6.$ *Result:* $3x + 6.$

11. *Subtract 50:* $-4x = -32.$ *Divide by* -4: $x = 8.$ *Check:* $50 - 4(8) = 50 - 32 = 18\ \checkmark.$

12. *Area* $= 7(x + 3) = 56.$ *Divide by 7:* $x + 3 = 8.$ *Subtract 3:* $x = 5.$

13. *Add 7.5:* $2.5x = 17.5.$ *Divide by 2.5:* $x = 7.$ *Check:* $2.5(7) - 7.5 = 17.5 - 7.5 = 10\ \checkmark.$

14. *Correct steps: subtract 8* $\boxtimes -2x > 6.$ *Divide by* -2 *and flip:* $x < -3.$ *The student forgot to flip.*

15. *Subtract 5:* $-x > 3.$ *Multiply by* -1 *and flip:* $x < -3.$ *Open circle at* $-3,$ *shade left.*

16. *Scale ratio:* $\frac{6}{2} = 3.$ *New dimensions:* $8 \times 3 = 24$ cm *and* $5 \times 3 = 15$ cm. *New perimeter:* $2(24 + 15) = 78$ cm.

17. *By the triangle inequality:* $12 - 8 <$ *third side* $< 12 + 8,$ *so* $4 <$ *third side* $< 20.$

18. *SAS produces a unique triangle. The included angle of* $90°$ *makes it a right triangle with legs 5 cm and 7 cm.*

19 A vertical cut through a cube perpendicular to the base typically produces a rectangle. If the cut goes through the center parallel to a face, it can be a square.

20 $r^2 = 12.56 \div 3.14 = 4$. So $r = 2$ m and $d = 4$ m.

21 Room: $14 \times 10 = 140$ ft^2. Closet: $3 \times 4 = 12$ ft^2. Remaining: $140 - 12 = 128$ ft^2.

22 $SA = 2(25 \times 18) + 2(25 \times 5) + 2(18 \times 5) = 900 + 250 + 180 = 1330$ cm^2.

23 First: $8 \times 5 \times 4 = 160$ in^3. Second: $10 \times 4 \times 4 = 160$ in^3. They have the same volume.

24 In a random sample, every member of the population has an equal chance of being chosen.

25 Dot plots show every data point, which is useful for small data sets where individual values matter.

26 There are 7 values. The middle value (4th) is 20.

27 If the bag contains only red and blue marbles, drawing a green marble is impossible ($P = 0$).

28 The probabilities are $0.4, 0.3, 0.2, 0.1$ — all different, so this is non-uniform. They sum to 1.0, making it valid.

29 $P(\text{tails}) = \frac{1}{2}$ and $P(\text{even}) = \frac{3}{6} = \frac{1}{2}$. $P = \frac{1}{2} \times \frac{1}{2} = \frac{1}{4}$. Or: 3 favorable out of 12 total outcomes.

30 A simulation uses random numbers, coins, dice, or spinners to model a real-world event and estimate probabilities.

✔ Practice Test 7 — Answer Key

Find more at
ViewMath.com/KS-Grade7

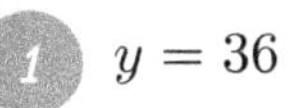 $y = 36$　　 D　　**3** 7 hours　　 D　　 $81.60　　**6** C　　 -3　　**8** B

9 B　　**10** A　　 $x = 9$　　**12** B　　**13** A　　**14** D　　**15** $x > 4$; open circle at 4, shade right

16 A　　**17** D　　**18** C　　**19** B　　**20** 39.25 cm^2　　**21** C　　**22** C　　**23** 180 cm^3　　**24** B

25 Class A　　**26** B　　**27** 15　　**28** B　　**29** B　　**30** C

💡 Time to Learn! 💡

Review the explanations below, **especially for the questions you missed**.

Understanding why each answer is correct builds stronger problem-solving skills.

Tip: Circle any questions you got wrong, then read their explanation carefully.

📖 Practice Test 7 — Detailed Explanations

1 $k = \frac{20}{5} = 4$. So $y = 4 \times 9 = 36$.

2 A proportional relationship always graphs as a straight line through the origin. It cannot be curved.

3 Rate: $42 \div 3 = 14$ mph. Time: $98 \div 14 = 7$ hours.

4 Divide the part by the percent: $9 \div 0.12 = 75$.

5 Fee: $85 \times 0.04 = \$3.40$. Seller receives: $85 - 3.40 = \$81.60$.

6 $\frac{|50-40|}{40} \times 100 = \frac{10}{40} \times 100 = 25\%$.

Find more at
ViewMath.com/KS-Grade7

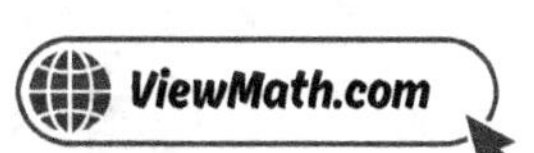

7 Moving 5 units left from 2: $2 - 5 = -3$.

8 $(-20) + 8 = -12$. Rising from a negative position adds a positive: $20 - 8 = 12$, keep negative.

9 "Twice a number" is $2n$. "6 more than" means add 6: $2n + 6$.

10 Combine: $\frac{3}{4}n - \frac{1}{4}n = \frac{2}{4}n = \frac{1}{2}n$. Add the constant: $\frac{1}{2}n + 5$.

11 Subtract 100: $-7x = -63$. Divide by -7: $x = 9$. Check: $100 - 7(9) = 100 - 63 = 37$ ✓.

12 The student wrote $3x + 4$ instead of $3x + 12$. Distributing correctly gives $3x + 12 = 30$.

13 Subtract $\frac{1}{2}$: $\frac{3}{4}b = 2\frac{1}{4} = \frac{9}{4}$. Multiply by $\frac{4}{3}$: $b = \frac{9}{4} \times \frac{4}{3} = 3$.

14 "No more than 25" means 25 or fewer. $x \leq 25$.

15 Subtract 4: $3x > 12$. Divide by 3: $x > 4$. Open circle at 4, shade right.

16 Scale ratio: $\frac{4}{8} = \frac{1}{2}$. New length: $10 \times \frac{1}{2} = 5$ cm. A larger scale (more real units per cm) shrinks the drawing.

17 The triangle inequality requires the sum of any two sides to be greater than the third. Here $3 + 4 = 7 < 8$, so no triangle can be formed.

18 AAA alone does not fix the size of the triangle. Many triangles can share these angle measures.

19 A vertical cut through the center of a cylinder produces a rectangle. The width equals the diameter and the height equals the cylinder's height.

20 $r = 5$ cm. Full circle: $3.14 \times 25 = 78.5$ cm^2. Semicircle: $78.5 \div 2 = 39.25$ cm^2.

21   Horizontal: $12 \times 2 = 24$ cm^2. Vertical: $2 \times 8 = 16$ cm^2. Total: $24 + 16 = 40$ cm^2.

22   Surface area is the total area covering the outside of a 3D object — the sum of the areas of all its faces.

23 $V = 9 \times 5 \times 4 = 180$ cm^3.

24   Selecting every 10th student from the school roster is systematic and gives all students a chance, making it the least biased.

25   Class A has a smaller IQR (6 vs. 14), meaning the middle 50% of scores are more tightly clustered.

26   A wider range indicates more variability, not better performance. Class A has a higher median and is more consistent (smaller IQR and range).

27   Point P is at 0.75. If $P(\text{red}) = 0.75$, then $0.75 \times 20 = 15$ red marbles.

28   A fair number cube has 6 equally likely outcomes, making it a uniform model.

29 $P(\text{heads}) = \frac{1}{2}$. Numbers greater than 4: $5, 6$, so $P = \frac{2}{6} = \frac{1}{3}$. $P = \frac{1}{2} \times \frac{1}{3} = \frac{1}{6}$.

30   A spinner with 4 equal sections has $\frac{1}{4} = 25\%$ chance for each section. Assigning one section as "win" gives 25%.

☑ Practice Test 8 — Answer Key

 B    2.4 miles    6 cm    D    About $18.60    C    B    C

Find more at
ViewMath.com/KS-Grade7

 B  Answers vary, e.g., $n + 3n + 7$ or $5n - n + 7$  A  A  $n = \dfrac{16}{5}$ or $3\dfrac{1}{5}$

 $9s + 35 \leq 200$; $s \leq 18$  $x > 2$; open circle at 2, shade right  3  4  C

 Any two of: square, rectangle, triangle, pentagon, hexagon  B  67.74 ft^2  B  C

 360  Yes; the means are about 2.5 to 3.3 MADs apart B 0.4 A $\dfrac{1}{12}$

B

💡 Time to Learn! 💡

Review the explanations below, **especially for the questions you missed**.

Understanding why each answer is correct builds stronger problem-solving skills.

Tip: Circle any questions you got wrong, then read their explanation carefully.

📖 Practice Test 8 — Detailed Explanations

1. $k = \dfrac{150}{2.5} = 60$ miles per hour.

2. Ava: $k = \dfrac{6}{5} = 1.2$ mph; at 6 hr. $1.2 \times 6 = 7.2$ mi. Ben: $k = \dfrac{4}{5} = 0.8$ mph; at 6 hr. $0.8 \times 6 = 4.8$ mi. Difference: $7.2 - 4.8 = 2.4$ miles.

3. $\dfrac{1}{4.5} = \dfrac{x}{27}$. Cross-multiply: $4.5x = 27$, so $x = 6$ cm.

4. $150\% = 1.50$. Multiply: $1.50 \times 40 = 60$. A percent greater than 100% gives a result greater than the whole.

5. Round to $93. Find 10%: $9.30. Double for 20%: $9.30 \times 2 = \$18.60$.

Find more at
ViewMath.com/KS-Grade7

6 $\frac{|35-40|}{40} \times 100 = \frac{5}{40} \times 100 = 12.5\%$.

7 Up 3 floors, then down 7: $3 + (-7) = -4$. The elevator is 4 floors below the lobby.

8 $(-50) + 75 = 25$. The deposit is larger than the overdraft, so the balance becomes positive.

9 Substitute: $-4(3) + 10 = -12 + 10 = -2$.

10 Any expression whose like terms combine to give $4n + 7$ is correct. For example: $n + 3n + 7 = 4n + 7$.

11 The pattern is $3x + 5$. Solve $3x + 5 = 41$: subtract 5 to get $3x = 36$, divide by 3: $x = 12$. Check: $3(12) + 5 = 41$ ✓.

12 Divide by 5: $n + 3 = -2$. Subtract 3: $n = -5$. Check: $5(-5 + 3) = 5(-2) = -10$ ✓.

13 Multiply every term by 6: $5n + 2 = 18$. Subtract 2: $5n = 16$. Divide by 5: $n = \frac{16}{5} = 3\frac{1}{5}$.

14 Total cost: $9s + 35 \leq 200$. Subtract 35: $9s \leq 165$. Divide by 9: $s \leq 18.\overline{3}$. Since s must be a whole number, $s \leq 18$.

15 Subtract 10: $-4x < -8$. Divide by -4 and flip: $x > 2$. Open circle at 2, shade right.

16 $24 \div 8 = 3$. Every old measurement is multiplied by 3 on the new map.

17 Factor pairs of 24: 1×24, 2×12, 3×8, 4×6. That is 4 different rectangles.

18 The third angle is $180° - 60° - 60° = 60°$. All angles are 60°, so the triangle is equilateral with all sides 5 cm.

Find more at
ViewMath.com/KS-Grade7

19 A cube can be sliced to produce squares, rectangles, triangles, pentagons, or hexagons depending on the angle and position of the cut.

20 The circle's diameter equals the side of the square: $d = 10$, so $r = 5$ cm. $A = \pi r^2 = 3.14 \times 25 = 78.5$ cm^2.

21 Patio: $12 \times 8 = 96$ ft^2. Hot tub: $\pi r^2 = 3.14 \times 9 = 28.26$ ft^2. Remaining: $96 - 28.26 = 67.74$ ft^2.

22 $SA = 2(5 \times 3) + 2(5 \times 2) + 2(3 \times 2) = 30 + 20 + 12 = 62$ cm^2.

23 $V = s^3 = 5^3 = 125$ m^3.

24 $\frac{6}{50} = 12\%$. Then 12% of $3{,}000 = 360$.

25 Difference $= 10$. Using MAD of 4: $\frac{10}{4} = 2.5$. Using MAD of 3: $\frac{10}{3} \approx 3.3$. Both are greater than 2, so the difference is meaningful.

26 $Q_1 = 22$, $Q_3 = 32$. IQR $= 32 - 22 = 10$.

27 2 favorable sections (blue, green) out of 5 total. $P = \frac{2}{5} = 0.4$.

28 Predicted: $\frac{5}{10} = 0.5$. Experimental: $\frac{24}{40} = 0.6$. The small difference is expected from natural variation.

29 $P(\text{tails}) = \frac{1}{2}$, $P(1) = \frac{1}{6}$. $P = \frac{1}{2} \times \frac{1}{6} = \frac{1}{12}$.

30 More trials produce more reliable estimates. The experimental probability approaches the theoretical value as trials increase.

✅ Practice Test 9 — Answer Key

1 A	**2** B	**3** C	**4** C	**5** C	**6** C	**7** B	**8** $-2°C$	**9** A

10 $12x + 8$ **11** B   **12** A   **13** C   **14** C   **15** A   **16** C   **17** D   **18** B

19 B   **20** C   **21** B   **22** C   **23** B   **24** C   **25** D   **26** B   **27** C   **28** B

29 C   **30** Roll the die; let 1 and 2 represent the event (or any 2 numbers out of 6)

💡 Time to Learn! 💡

Review the explanations below, *especially for the questions you missed*.

Understanding why each answer is correct builds stronger problem-solving skills.

Tip: Circle any questions you got wrong, then read their explanation carefully.

📖 Practice Test 9 — Detailed Explanations

1 By convention, $k = \frac{y}{x} = \frac{20}{8} = 2.5$. Student B computed $\frac{x}{y}$, which is the reciprocal — not k.

2 The point $(1, 5)$ means $x = 1$ ticket and $y = \$5$, so one ticket costs $5. This is the unit rate.

3 Rate: $120 \div 8 = 15$ pages/min. Time for 450: $450 \div 15 = 30$ min.

4 Divide the part by the whole: $14 \div 56 = 0.25 = 25\%$.

5 $55 \times 1.20 = \$66.00$.

Find more at
ViewMath.com/KS-Grade7

6 $\frac{|8,000-7,500|}{7,500} \times 100 = \frac{500}{7,500} \times 100 \approx 6.67\%$.

7 $7 - 7 = 0$. Note that $|-7| - |7| = 7 - 7 = 0$ also works, but since only one answer is expected, B is the most direct additive-inverse example. Actually D also equals 0. But B is the clearest demonstration of opposites.

8 Start at $-3°C$. Rise $4°$: $-3 + 4 = 1°C$. Drop $3°$: $1 + (-3) = -2°C$.

9 $5n$ means "5 times a number." Subtracting 8 means "8 less than" that product.

10 Perimeter $= 2(4x - 1) + 2(2x + 5) = 8x - 2 + 4x + 10 = 12x + 8$.

11 Substitute $x = 5$: $4(5) + 3 = 20 + 3 = 23$. So $4x + 3 = 23$ is correct.

12 Divide both sides by 2: $x + 6 = 10$. Subtract 6: $x = 4$. Check: $2(4 + 6) = 2(10) = 20$ ✓.

13 Sale price is $\frac{2}{3}p$. After the \$5 coupon: $\frac{2}{3}p - 5 = 15$.

14 Subtract 6: $-3n \leq -6$. Divide by -3 and flip the sign: $n \geq 2$.

15 Add 3: $\frac{x}{2} > 4$. Multiply by 2: $x > 8$. Open circle at 8, shade right.

16 Scale ratio: $\frac{12}{4} = 3$. New width: $0.5 \times 3 = 1.5$ in.

17 The sides must add to 12. Many dimension pairs work: 1×11, 2×10, 3×9, etc. Perimeter alone does not fix the rectangle.

18 Two sides and the angle between them is the SAS (Side-Angle-Side) condition.

19 A vertical cut through the apex of a cone produces a triangle (specifically an isosceles triangle).

20 Full circle area $= \pi r^2 = 3.14 \times 64 = 200.96 \ cm^2$. Quarter circle $= 200.96 \div 4 = 50.24 \ cm^2$.

21 Rectangle: $6 \times 4 = 24 \ cm^2$. Triangle: $\frac{1}{2} \times 6 \times 2 = 6 \ cm^2$. Total: $24 + 6 = 30 \ cm^2$.

22 A cube has 6 faces. $SA = 6s^2 = 6 \times 16 = 96 \ cm^2$.

23 $V = Bh = 24 \times 7 = 168 \ cm^3$.

24 The sample is the smaller group chosen from the population — the 100 students measured.

25 Class A median $= 78$, Class B median $= 65$. Class A's range (60–95) overlaps with Class B's range (50–80), but Class A is higher overall.

26 Group A range $= 20$, Group B range $= 60$. Group B's data is far more spread out.

27 There are $3 + 5 + 2 = 10$ marbles total. Blue $= 5$. $P = \frac{5}{10} = \frac{1}{2}$. Both B and C are equivalent, but $\frac{5}{10}$ directly matches the bar graph reading.

28 Predicted: $\frac{1}{4} = 0.25$. Observed: $\frac{25}{80} = 0.3125$. They are close, which supports the model.

29 Only one outcome out of 8 is all tails (TTT). $P = \frac{1}{8}$.

30 Choose 2 of the 6 faces to represent the event. $P = \frac{2}{6} = \frac{1}{3}$.

✔ Practice Test 10 — Answer Key

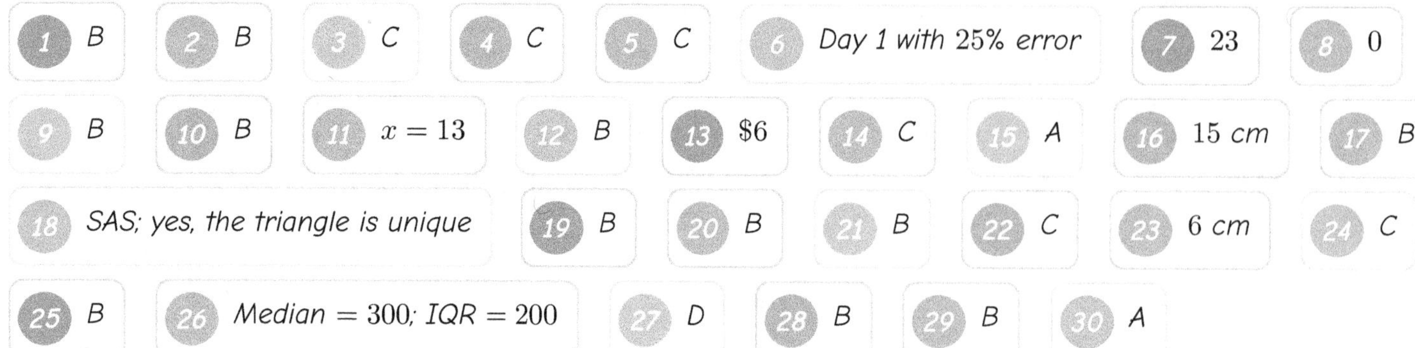

| 1 | B | 2 | B | 3 | C | 4 | C | 5 | C | 6 | Day 1 with 25% error | 7 | 23 | 8 | 0 |

| 9 | B | 10 | B | 11 | $x = 13$ | 12 | B | 13 | $6 | 14 | C | 15 | A | 16 | 15 cm | 17 | B |

| 18 | SAS; yes, the triangle is unique | 19 | B | 20 | B | 21 | B | 22 | C | 23 | 6 cm | 24 | C |

| 25 | B | 26 | Median $= 300$; IQR $= 200$ | 27 | D | 28 | B | 29 | B | 30 | A |

💡 Time to Learn! 💡

*Review the explanations below, **especially for the questions you missed.***

Understanding why each answer is correct builds stronger problem-solving skills.

***Tip:** Circle any questions you got wrong, then read their explanation carefully.*

📖 Practice Test 10 — Detailed Explanations

1. Use any labeled point: $k = \frac{2}{3}$ from $(3, 2)$. Check: $\frac{4}{6} = \frac{2}{3}$ ✓.

2. The point $(1, 9)$ directly gives the unit rate: 9 miles per hour. Check: $\frac{27}{3} = 9$ and $\frac{45}{5} = 9$ ✓.

3. Set up a proportion: $\frac{2}{15} = \frac{7}{d}$. Cross-multiply: $2d = 105$, so $d = 52.5$ miles.

4. $35\% = 0.35$. Multiply: $0.35 \times 480 = 168$ fiction books.

5. Each share: $70 \div 2 = \$35$. Tip: $35 \times 0.15 = \$5.25$. Total each: $35 + 5.25 = \$40.25$.

6. Day 1: $|10 - 8|/8 = 25\%$. Day 2: $|6 - 5|/5 = 20\%$. Day 3: $|8 - 10|/10 = 20\%$. Day 1 has the largest percent error at 25%.

Find more at
ViewMath.com/KS-Grade7

7 The absolute value of -23 is its distance from 0, which is 23.

8 -18 and 18 are additive inverses (opposites). Their sum is always 0.

9 Substitute: $2(-3) + 7 = -6 + 7 = 1$.

10 Combine variable terms: $3y - 5y = -2y$. Combine constants: $8 - 2 = 6$. Result: $-2y + 6$.

11 The model shows $3x + 6 = 45$. Subtract 6: $3x = 39$. Divide by 3: $x = 13$.

12 Distribute: $8x - 6 = 26$. Add 6: $8x = 32$. Divide by 8: $x = 4$. Check: $2(4 \cdot 4 - 3) = 2(13) = 26$ ✓.

13 Student $C = \frac{1}{2} \times 12 = \$6$. Check: Student $B = 31.50 - 12 - 6 = \$13.50$. Total: $12 + 13.50 + 6 = 31.50$ ✓.

14 Subtract 9: $-x \leq 6$. Multiply by -1 and flip: $x \geq -6$.

15 Subtract 6: $-2x \leq -10$. Divide by -2 and flip: $x \geq 5$. Closed circle at 5, shade right.

16 Scale ratio: $\frac{12}{4} = 3$. New length: $5 \times 3 = 15$ cm.

17 All circles with radius 5 cm are congruent — they have the same shape and size. In terms of the figure itself (ignoring position), there is exactly one such circle.

18 Two sides (8 cm and 6 cm) and the included angle (65°) give the SAS condition. SAS always produces exactly one unique triangle.

19 A diagonal plane that passes through all six faces of a cube creates a regular hexagonal cross-section.

20 $A = \pi r^2 = \frac{22}{7} \times 49 = 154 \; in^2$.

21 Rectangle: $10 \times 4 = 40 \; cm^2$. Triangle: $\frac{1}{2} \times 10 \times 3 = 15 \; cm^2$. Total: $40 + 15 = 55 \; cm^2$.

22 $SA = 2(30 \times 20) + 2(30 \times 6) + 2(20 \times 6) = 1200 + 360 + 240 = 1{,}800 \; cm^2$.

23 $360 = 12 \times w \times 5 = 60w$. $w = 360 \div 60 = 6 \; cm$.

24 Average the two samples: $\frac{18+22}{2} = 20$ out of $50 = 40\%$. Then 40% of $1{,}000 = 400$.

25 The median is less affected by skew than the mean, so it is the best measure to compare a skewed and a symmetric distribution.

26 Median (3rd value) $= 300$. $Q_1 = 200$, $Q_3 = 400$. $IQR = 400 - 200 = 200$.

27 A probability of 1 means the event will definitely happen — it is certain.

28 Red covers half the spinner ($180°$), while Blue and Green each cover a quarter ($90°$ each). This is a non-uniform model.

29 Pairs with product 12: $(2,6), (6,2), (3,4), (4,3)$ — that is 4 out of 36. $P = \frac{4}{36} = \frac{1}{9}$.

30 $P(sum = 7) = \frac{6}{36} = \frac{1}{6}$. Expected: $36 \times \frac{1}{6} = 6$. The simulation gave 8, slightly above expected.

Well done checking your answers!

Keep practicing to strengthen your skills.

Find more at
ViewMath.com/KS-Grade7

Author's Final Note

I hope you enjoyed this book as much as I enjoyed writing it. Whether you are a student working through the material, a parent supporting your child's learning, or a teacher guiding your class, I have tried to make this book as clear and engaging as possible. I hope I have succeeded. If you have any suggestions for improvement, please let me know. I would love to hear from you.

The accuracy of calculations is very important to me. We have done our best, but I also expect that I have made some minor errors. Constant improvement is the name of the game. If you find any errors, please let me know. I will fix them in the next edition.

For students: Your learning journey does not end here. I have written a series of books to help you learn math. Make sure you browse through them. I especially recommend workbooks and practice tests to help you prepare for your exams.

For parents: Thank you for investing in your child's education. I encourage you to explore the companion resources available online to help support your child outside the classroom.

For teachers: Thank you for the invaluable work you do every day. I hope this book serves as a useful resource in your classroom. Feel free to reach out if you have suggestions or would like to discuss how best to use this book with your students.

I also enjoy reading your reviews. If you have a moment, please leave a review on where you found this book. It will help others find this book. If you have any questions or comments, please feel free to contact me at DrNazari@ViewMath.com.

And one last thing: Remember to use online resources for additional help. I recommend using the resources on https://ViewMath.com You can find video lessons, practice problems, and more. You can also use the online companion for this book to track your progress and access additional resources.

Wishing all students the best in their studies, parents every success in supporting their children, and teachers continued inspiration in their classrooms!

Dr. A. Nazari

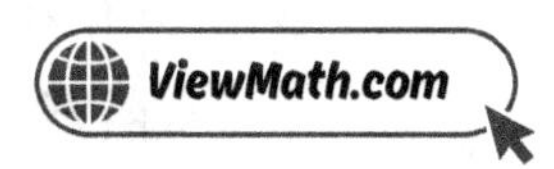

Great Job! Keep Learning with ViewMath!

*Keep up the great work! Visit **viewmath.com/KS-Grade7** for free lessons, quizzes, and more.*

Study Guide

Workbook

Step-by-Step

3 Practice Tests

5 Practice Tests

7 Practice Tests

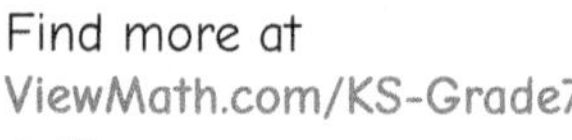
Find more at
ViewMath.com/KS-Grade7